Published in 1998 by Icon Books Ltd,
Grange Road, Duxford, Cambridge CB2 4QF
e-mail: icon@mistral.co.uk

Distributed in the UK, Europe, Canada, South Africa and Asia
by the Penguin Group:
Penguin Books Ltd, 27 Wrights Lane, London W8 5TZ

Published in Australia in 1998 by Allen & Unwin Pty Ltd,
PO Box 8500, 9 Atchison Street, St. Leonards, NSW 2065

ISBN 1 84046 029 6

Series edited by Sport and Leisure Books Ltd
Layout and illustrations: Zoran Jevtic, Audiografix
Cover design by Zoran Jevtic and Jeremy Cox
Photographs supplied by Allsport

Printed and bound in Great Britain by
Biddles Ltd, Guildford and King's Lynn

CONTENTS

INTRODUCTION

Boxing is an improbable obsession for a white, middle-aged and middle-class man whose own athletic abilities never extended much beyond a mean forehand smash in the Civil Service Table Tennis League thirty years ago, but the sport is undiscriminating about its victims. Once you're hooked, often against all logic and common sense, there is no escape, and when you cover the sport from the privileged close-up view I have enjoyed since the late 1960s, you wouldn't have it any other way.

I saw my first live boxing around 1954, when I was seven or eight and an amateur show was staged in the *Palais de Danse* at the end of the Promenade in my home town of Portstewart, Co. Derry. (The Palais still stands, but the old hall where everybody from Adam Faith to Jim Reeves performed is now owned, incongruously, by the Dominican nuns and forms part of their College.)

The exploits of Derry featherweight Billy 'Spider' Kelly had already caught my attention, but I never thought it likely that I would actually see a live boxing show, since such things were unheard-of in Portstewart. When the tournament was announced, I despaired because the ticket prices – ringside 7/6, or 37 1/2p – were far beyond my budget on a weekly allowance of a shilling (5p). But my father knew how keen I was, and treated me to a ringside seat.

I was captivated, instantly, and the journey that began in the Palais has, over the subsequent forty-odd years, taken me to rather grander venues like Madison Square Garden, the New Orleans Superdome, the Olympic Auditorium in Los Angeles, more Las Vegas arenas than I can recall, and a host of others ranging from a baseball park in Mexico to the splendid Sun City in South Africa. Locked away for six years as a boarder in St Patrick's College, Armagh (1957–63), I nurtured my obsession for the sport by having a day-boy smuggle in the weekly *Boxing News*. From the age of eleven, when I first discovered *Boxing News*, my sole ambition in life was to edit the paper. My contemporaries dreamt of athletic glory, or unlimited success with girls, but I was sustained by hold-the-front-page fantasies.

Incredibly, I made it. I came to England in 1963, to take up a stupefyingly boring position in the Civil Service, but by 1967 I had got as far as the press benches at the Albert Hall where I covered the activities of Irish boxers on the show for the Belfast *Irish News*. I gradually spread my freelance net, including contributing to *Boxing News* and its later short-lived rival *Boxing World*, until in 1974 Graham Houston, then editor of *Boxing News*, offered me a staff position. The wages were even less than the Civil Service, but I would have paid them for the privilege of working there.

In August 1977 Graham emigrated to Canada, and my impossible dream came true: I succeeded him as editor, and held the job for nineteen years. I like to think that I never did an honest day's work in all that time, because I could never take seriously the fact that people paid me well to travel the world and watch, from the best seats in the house, fights for which I would happily buy a ticket.

I stepped down, with extreme reluctance, in October 1996, since when I have been a full-time freelance, mainly with the *Independent on Sunday*, *Total Sport* and most recently, with the new all-sports Sunday broadsheet, *Sport First*. The love affair that began forty-four years ago in that old dance hall is still as passionate as ever, and has given me a wonderfully enjoyable and fulfilling career.

Your own involvement in the sport may not have been so intimate: perhaps you are one of the new breed of fan, lured to the game by the extravagant showmanship of Chris Eubank or Naseem Hamed. You have only to look around you when either of those two performs to see how far removed their public are from the sport's traditional market. It is a fair bet that you won't be seeing the same faces next Saturday night at York Hall, Bethnal Green, the game's spiritual home in East London.

After years of struggling with a down-market image, boxing is suddenly fashionable and your ringside seat at York Hall is now likely to be occupied by a style writer from *Arena* or *The Face*. Boxing is cool, its profile raised by blanket and highly professional coverage on satellite TV. If you have a dish, or cable TV, you can watch top quality boxing most weekends, and excellent magazine programmes like Sky Sports' *Ringside* help bring the fighters to life and give them an extra dimension.

Boxing may be more accessible than ever, but don't be fooled into thinking that it is an easy sport to understand, or to follow. I have tried to keep the tone of this book as much entertainment as educational, aware always of the complexities of the problems presented to newcomers to the sport by the myriad of controlling bodies and conflicting interests.

I don't understand the half of it myself, after deriving my day-to-day living solely from boxing for the last twenty-four years, so don't feel downhearted if you can't immediately tell your WBO from your IBF. What you ought to be able to do, at least after reading the section on today's stars, is to drop in conversation-stoppers about the likes of Saman Sorjaturong or Dariusz Michalczewski whenever discussion of Hamed's latest triumph gets boring.

I hope that your voyage of discovery through the fascinating world of boxing will be as enjoyable as was mine, and for that I have to thank Graham Houston for giving me that long-craved opportunity all those years ago. This book is dedicated to him, in long overdue appreciation of a fine writer and a cherished friend.

Harry Mullan
Bridge, Kent, April 1998

THE PRIZE RING

Naseem Hamed is unlikely to have read the *Iliad*, so he is probably unaware that when he made his much-publicised promise to send opponent Tom Johnson 'back home in a coffin' in 1997 he was echoing a speech by Homer's champion, Epeus. 'I'm going to tear the fellow's flesh to ribbons and smash his bones', Epeus brags in best pre-fight press conference style. 'I recommend him to have all his mourners standing by to take him off when I've done with him'. The subsequent description of his showdown with Euryalus, written around 1100 BC, is the earliest known ringside report, and the old hack captured the flavour of the occasion as surely as he did the participants.

There was bare-knuckle fighting in the original Olympics in ancient Greece, and it was also a regular entertainment in Rome. Predictably, the most combative race in Europe, the Celts, were at it too. Between 632 BC and 1169 AD, a kind of Celtic Olympiad was staged periodically at the tomb of Tailte, an Irish queen, about ten miles from Tara, the traditional seat of the High Kings of Ireland. Known as the Tailteann Games, the events included boxing and, unlike the brutal fights to the death with iron-studded hand bindings called *caesti* which featured in Roman gladiatorial arenas, the Celtic form was a simple test of stamina, courage and athletic ability.

The sport seems to have died out, and does not reappear until the late seventeenth century. The *Protestant Mercury* has the improbable distinction of being the first publication to record a fight result, when its January 1681 edition carried an account of 'a match of boxing before His Grace the Duke of Albemarle, between the Duke's footman and a butcher.' The butcher is described as 'an experienced boxer', so bare-knuckling must have existed in some form at the time.

James Figg, the first English champion, opened his famous boxing academy in London in 1719, and quickly acquired an impressive list of high society patrons whose backing gave the game a kind of respectability. By 1723 it had become so popular that King George I ordered a ring to be erected in Hyde Park for public use, and twenty years later Figg's successor as champion, Jack Broughton, published the first Prize Ring Rules which governed the sport until the London Prize Ring Rules were established in 1838.

In the interim, the game fell into disrepute through an unsavoury series of fixed fights and fatalities, before it was rescued by a string of outstanding performers like Daniel Mendoza, Gentleman John Jackson, the freed American slave Tom Molineaux and the Bristol hero Tom Cribb, who became the ring's first superstar. He drew crowds of 30,000 or more, and attracted royal patronage.

But by 1837, when the dour Victoria came to the throne, Britain was in the grip of a religious revival led by the new evangelical movement, and the raucous, bawdy world of the ring had no place in that society. Boxing carried on and even produced a few major figures like Tom Sayers and Bendigo and Big Ben Caunt, but the last English bare-knuckler of note, Jem Mace, had to go to America, Australia and New Zealand to earn a living at his trade.

The Queensberry Rules were drawn up in 1867 to govern both the prize ring and the growing sport of amateur boxing, which was conducted with

**THOMAS
MOLINEAUX**

Born in Georgetown in 1784, but most of his early life was spent in Virginia. He was 5ft. 8½ins. in height and weighed 13 stone 3 lb. A most formidable boxer, he was not very successful in his boxing career, yet came very near to being Champion of England. Died in Ireland, August, 1818, at the age of 34.

'mufflers' (gloves.) The balance of power shifted West, as the flood of European and particularly Irish immigrants brought their love of the game with them to America. John Carmel Heenan, whose descendant of the same name became the Cardinal of Westminster in the 1960s, was the first American to earn an international reputation in the ring, and he was followed by other Irish-Americans like Jake Kilrain, Paddy Ryan and John L. Sullivan, who became the last of the bare-knuckle champs when he stopped Ryan in nine rounds in 1882.

Sullivan held the title under Prize Ring Rules until 1892, when he accepted the challenge of a San Francisco bank clerk called James J. Corbett. 'The Queensberry rules must govern this contest', he stipulated, 'as I want fighting, not foot-racing.' That decision spelt the end of the bare-knuckle era: when Corbett knocked out the veteran in the twenty-first round of the sport's first gloved championship contest, the game changed forever.

EARLY DAYS IN BRITAIN

The first attempt to organise boxing in Britain in any recognisable, modern sense came with the foundation of the Pelican Club in London in 1887. It existed mainly as a gambling house, catering for wealthy aristocrats with more money than sense, and so was never short of customers. The Club organised regular bare-knuckle tournaments, which were strictly illegal, but the authorities turned a blind eye to the Pelican's activities while continuing to enforce the law against boxers and promoters who operated without the Club's upper-class protection. In 1890, with bare-knuckle fighting dropping out of favour, the Pelican produced its own set of rules modelled on

TOM CRIBB

Born at Gloucester, 1781. At one time Champion of England. He stood 5ft. 10ins. and weighed 14 stone. Went to London at the age of 13, and became a bell-hanger. Later he took up coal-heaving and this gained him the name of the Black Diamond. He was, beyond doubt, the most famous and popular of the old-time champions. He died in Woolwich, May, 1848, and a monument was erected to his memory.

Queensberry's, which set the maximum number of rounds at twenty and the minimum weight for gloves at six ounces.

In 1891 the National Sporting Club (NSC) was formed by two well-known sportsmen, John Fleming and A.F. 'Peggy' Bettinson, with a view to providing similar facilities for those customers a little lower down on the elaborate Victorian social scale. It started life as a dinner club, where members could eat and drink at the NSC's Covent Garden headquarters before enjoying the boxing. Fleming and Bettinson persuaded so many of the Pelican's members to change their allegiance that, in 1892, the Pelican went out of business and left the NSC as the undisputed master of British boxing.

The Club's newly-acquired aristocratic backing helped smooth the scandals when three boxers died in fights there between 1897 and 1899, but when a fourth fatality happened in 1901, eight of those involved, including the NSC officials, were charged with manslaughter. Their acquittal at the Old Bailey established the important legal principle that death resulting from an accident in a properly-supervised sporting contest was not a crime, and effectively the verdict legalised the sport in practice if not in statute.

The NSC revised the Pelican's rules in 1909 and again in 1923, underlining their position as the sport's quasi-official governing body. They introduced Lonsdale Belts for British championships in 1909, and thereafter only contests promoted by the NSC could be regarded as 'official' title fights. The Club ruled the game with an autocratic hand: the 'Gentlemen and Players' ethos was strictly enforced, and their

TOM SAYERS

Born 1826, at Brighton. He was of medium height and weighed under 11 stone. He was a wonderful fighter and possessed great courage, skill and ringcraft. Many of his victorious fights were against men much bigger than himself. He was a real Champion of England, and was only beaten once during his short career. He died at the age of 39, in 1865.

monopoly on championships meant that they could keep boxers' purses low. Jack Johnson, the first black world heavyweight champion, ruffled their aristocratic feathers when he demanded payment in advance, and in cash, for an appearance there: the distinguished committee were not accustomed to having their financial integrity questioned, and although they paid up as Johnson stipulated, they made sure that he never boxed there again and that he would not enjoy their support in his campaign for a world title shot.

The Club did not have a monopoly on promotions, though, and working-class London arenas like the Blackfriars Ring, Premierland and Wonderland ran regular shows featuring the leading stars of the day. The Ring, built as a Nonconformist chapel, was circular in shape so that the Devil would not have a corner to hide in. It became the country's most famous arena (under the direction first of the former lightweight champion Dick Burge and later his widow, Bella). The Ring continued to run two or even three shows a week until a German bomb finally knocked it out in October 1940.

For prestige promotions, the Holland Park Arena and the Albert Hall, where Jeff Dickson brought American-style flair to the British game, were favourite. Boxing flourished in the provinces too, particularly in the Midlands, and resentment began to grow amongst commercial promoters at the degree of control exercised by the NSC. The Club was caught in a clear conflict of interest: it had to decide whether it wished to be the sport's controlling body, in which case it could not sit in judgement on fellow-promoters; or whether it wished to continue promoting, in which case it would have to relinquish any claim to administer boxing.

TOMMY FARR

A Welshman, who became Heavy-weight Champion of Great Britain and the Empire in 1937, by beating Ben Foord. After defeating Max Baer, the former Heavy weight Champion of the world, in London, he went to America and met Joe Louis for the Heavy-weight Championship of the world, and was narrowly beaten on points. Farr who has now relinquished his British Heavy-weight title has made a fortune from his profession.

Eventually, the Board of Control (BBBC), which had first been set up as a puppet of the NSC's in 1918, came to represent instead the promoters who worked outside the NSC, and as the Board's support grew, so the influence of the NSC declined until, in 1929, they renounced all administrative claims and the Board reconstituted itself as the sport's formal governing body.

Shortly afterwards, the NSC withdrew from promoting and ceased to be a force in British boxing. Although the club, in various incarnations, continued to run regular Monday night shows at the Cafe Royal, Regent Street, until the 1980s, it was by then just another dinner-boxing club, boasting barely an echo of former glories.

THE COLOUR BAR

The NSC's unhappy experience with Jack Johnson had soured them against black fighters in general, and their attitude was summarised by the Club matchmaker 'Peggy' Bettinson. 'We have no prejudice against the Negro fighter', he said in a variation of the old 'Some of my best friends' line, 'but we would not run the risk of having to suffer another Jack Johnson.'

Black boxers had already played a significant part in the sport's development. Two of the leading Prize Ring attractions, Bill Richmond and Tom Molineaux, were former American slaves, and a black South African, Andrew Jeptha, was briefly British welterweight champion in 1907. But after Johnson, the barriers were up, and to their lasting shame the new Board of Control enshrined prejudice in the rule book. In the minutes of the 1929 meeting which established the Board, and

BENNY LYNCH
Born at Glasgow April 2nd, 1914. He won the British, European and World's Fly-weight Championships by knocking out the Holder of these titles, Jackie Brown in two rounds at Manchester Sept. 9th, 1935. He successfully defended his titles against all comers until June 29th, 1938, when he met Jackie Jurich, of America, at Paisley. Lynch was over-weight and had to forfeit all his three titles.

which were supposedly endorsed by Lord Lonsdale himself, the words 'of British nationality' were replaced by 'of white parents' in the qualifying criteria for those wishing to contest the British title.

That killed the hopes of Britain's black boxers, of whom the most notable was Manchester middleweight Len Johnson. His ninety-two victims included champions like Ted 'Kid' Lewis, Roland Todd, Len Harvey, Ted Moore and Harry Crossley, but the closest he got to a title was a 1932 rematch with Harvey which was billed as being for the British title, but which the Board refused to recognise on the grounds of Johnson's mixed-race parentage.

The Board's long-serving General Secretary, Charles Donmall, attempted to defend the indefensible by arguing that, 'it is only right that a small country such as ours should have championships restricted to boxers of white parents – otherwise we might be faced with a situation where all our British titles are held by coloured Empire boxers'. Even at the time, that attitude did not command much respect, and the notable contribution made by black servicemen in the Second World War strengthened the abolitionist case.

Questions were raised at government level in 1946, and a campaign backed by a number of prominent sportswriters finally paid off in 1947 when the infamous 'Colour Bar' was lifted. When a year later, in June 1948, Randolph Turpin's older brother Dick defeated Vince Hawkins to become the first black man to win a British title under the auspices of the BBBC, he earned a place in British boxing history which, in the long term, would be of even more significance than Randolph's world title win over Sugar Ray Robinson in July 1951.

BOOM AND BUST

The years after the Second World War saw boxing become one of the most popular sports in Britain, with promoter Jack Solomons drawing huge crowds to outdoor shows featuring the likes of Freddie Mills and Bruce Woodcock. As well as the big White City promotions, there were regular tournaments at Harringay Arena, the Albert Hall and – less frequently – the Empire Pool, Wembley. Boxing flourished because it offered cheap entertainment, and even if the purses were not huge, for the boxers at least there was no shortage of earning opportunities.

But by the end of the 1940s the boom was already slowing, as devaluation of the pound cut the number of international stars appearing in British rings. An entertainment tax of 16 per cent was imposed on promotions, which forced ticket prices up and had a corresponding effect on sales, but the near-fatal blow fell in August 1952, when the tax was more than doubled, to 33 1/3 per cent. The effect was immediate, and dramatic.

Many small promoters simply dropped out of the business, while those who struggled on usually did so at a loss. The Stewards of the BBBC were so concerned that they petitioned the Chancellor to revert to 16 per cent, to no avail, and by 1953 the total number of promotions in Britain had dropped by 60 per cent from its high-water mark in 1948. The Chancellor remained unmoved, although a few lucky promoters gained some consolation in the second half of 1954 as TV began to take an interest in the sport.

The arrival of commercial TV in 1956 brought more money into the business, as the new channel was

LEN HARVEY
Born at Helston, Cornwall 1907, he has the distinction of being the only boxer in history to win the British Championship in the Middle, Light-Heavy and Heavy-weight classes. He won the Middle-weight title in 1929, the Light-Heavy weight in 1937, and the Heavy-weight, including the Empire Title, with a victory over Jack Petersen.

quick to appreciate that boxing made cheap and entertaining TV, but the tax remained in force until Chancellor Peter Thorneycroft abolished it in 1957.

That was good news for those few who had managed to keep going, but the face of British boxing had been changed for ever as many of the small halls – usually local swimming baths – no longer hosted boxing. This type of venue had been an important breeding ground for new talent, places where young boxers could learn their trade away from the spotlight and where the occasional defeat would not be regarded as the end of the world. Taken together with the demise of the boxing booths in travelling fairs, where so many stars of earlier generations had served their apprenticeships, the decline of the small halls had a disastrous effect.

By the 1960s Jack Solomons was a spent force, and the major shows were run almost exclusively by a London grouping whose membership changed to include at various times Harry Levene, Mike Barrett and Terry Lawless, with matchmaker Mickey Duff and financier (and former manager) Jarvis Astaire ever-present. The Board of Control operated a policy of not permitting major shows to take place in London within two weeks of each other, and the group exploited the loophole by booking most of the available dates for shows alternating between the Albert Hall and Wembley, thus effectively gaining a monopoly on big-time promotions. Even those small halls which still functioned, like Shoreditch Town Hall and Bethnal Green, were satellites of the group, with Duff and later Lawless acting as matchmaker and/or promoter at the East London venues.

As the number of promotions dwindled, fewer and

fewer boxers came into the sport. In the early 1950s there were more than 2,000 licensed professionals, but in 1971 only 291 British boxers (including British-based Commonwealth fighters) saw action. Boxing was on the ropes – and it was only saved by a return to the gas-light and hansom cab days of the National Sporting Club. Dinner-boxing clubs sprang up across the country. Every major city had at least one, and so too did places like Southend, Stoke-on-Trent and Solihull.

Without exception they were black-tie, men-only functions, usually featuring an after-dinner comedian followed by three or four fights of indifferent quality. Some, like the Anglo-American Sporting Club (A-ASC) in London or the revived NSC, had a big enough budget to stage occasional championship fights, and the A-ASC gave the ageing Sugar Ray Robinson his only win in a British ring when he stopped the Nigerian Johnny Angel, at the tail-end of his fabulous career.

The sporting club bubble burst eventually, partly because the influx of TV money in the early 1980s made commercial shows viable again, and also because – political correctness aside – the public began to realise that it was wrong to discriminate against women so blatantly. Boxing is no longer an exclusively male preserve, but however objectionable and chauvinistic the concept of men-only sporting clubs seems in the 1990s, there is little doubt that they saved the game from extinction in the 1970s.

WARREN CASHES IN

The ruthlessly competitive nature of boxing promoting means, inevitably, that only the most able operators survive. Jeff Dickson had dominated the 1920s, Jack Solomons the 1940s and 1950s, Mickey Duff the 1960s and 1970s, but the 1980s and 1990s belonged to Frank Warren. Most of his predecessors had a background in the sport – Duff had nearly seventy pro fights, and even Solomons had a brief and unsuccessful experience in the ring – but when Warren burst onto the scene in the early 1980s it was from an unusual quarter. He had been running 'pirate' shows outside the Board's jurisdiction, and made such a success of it that he began to pose a real threat to the established order.

He was the driving force behind the National Boxing Council, which licensed its own promoters and published regular newsletters lambasting the Board and the boxing press for their reluctance to cover their activities. The Board at that time were members only of the World Boxing Council, so the NBC sought membership of the rival World Boxing Association (WBA), whose policy was to recognise only one 'governing body' from each member country. To head off the threat this would have posed, the Board promptly joined the WBA and invited Warren to take out a BBBC licence, presumably adopting LBJ's theory that it is better to have a perceived trouble-maker 'inside the tent pissing out than outside the tent pissing in'.

They soon regretted it, as Warren used the process of law to challenge and overturn all the Board's restrictive practices, including the fourteen-day rule controlling the frequency of major promotions and the policy of not permitting championships to be televised live. The string of expensively-won judgements in his favour shattered the old

Frank Warren

monopolistic structure, and when he lured ITV into British boxing by offering them the unlikely carrot of televising yet another comeback by Joe Bugner, he was on his way.

He formed a series of short-term alliances with assorted provincial promoters, whose shows would be screened on their local commercial channel, while his major shows were networked live on ITV. Previously, ITV had only screened American boxing, usually on a next-day delayed basis. The Mickey Duff group had a lucrative deal with BBC, running their shows on a Tuesday night to facilitate inclusion in the BBC's Wednesday *Sportsnight* slot, and because only they could guarantee a young fighter TV exposure they tended to attract the best and brightest of the new faces.

Warren's ITV deal changed that, and he went on to sign up a host of future world champions like Terry Marsh, Nigel Benn, Colin McMillan,

Nigel Benn (right) on the way to victory over the ill-fated Gerald McClellan in their WBC world title fight

Naseem Hamed, Steve Robinson and – late in their careers – Steve Collins and Frank Bruno. His promotions attracted huge viewing figures: Nigel Benn's thrilling but ultimately catastrophic clash with Gerald McClellan drew 13 million viewers, more even than the Grand National.

Ironically, that fight was also Warren's last major show on ITV: shortly afterwards, he completed a fabulous deal with Sky Sports, using the trump card of his alliance with the leading American promoter, Don King, which afforded access to Mike Tyson's comeback. The partnership with King did not survive, but the deal with Sky has and, built around the spectacular talent of Naseem Hamed, has ushered in the era of pay-per-view TV in Britain.

GHETTO BLASTERS

Boxing has always been the sport of the ghettos, the escape route for ambitious and athletically-gifted youngsters from the wrong side of the tracks. This has been particularly true in America, a country whose social history can be traced from a perusal of the list of boxing champions of the day.

The sport was brought there by European immigrants, principally Irish, and they and their descendants dominated the early years. John L. Sullivan and James J. Corbett held the heavyweight championship, and Tom Sharkey from Dundalk came close to it. George Gardner, Jack O'Brien, Mike McTigue, Jimmy Slattery, Tommy Loughran and Billy Conn were light-heavyweight kings, while middleweight champions of Irish birth or extraction included 'Nonpareil' Jack Dempsey, Tommy Ryan, Mike O'Dowd, Mickey Walker and Paul Pender. Jimmy McLarnin, Belfast-born and Canadian-

JAMES J. CORBETT

Actor and Boxer, always immaculate and looked the Champion born. Known sometimes as "Gentleman Jim." Formerly a Bank Clerk, he turned professional at 18, and became a supremely scientific fighting boxer. Born in San Francisco in 1866. At 26 he aspired to the Title, the fight taking place at New Orleans, for a purse of 25,000 dollars.

raised, was a brilliant welterweight and lightweight champion in the 1930s, while Terry McGovern ruled the bantamweight and featherweight division at the turn of the century. Modern-era fighters like Rinty Monaghan and Davy Larmour (flyweight), John Caldwell (bantam), Barry McGuigan (feather) and Steve Collins (middle and super-middle) have maintained a fine tradition.

As the Irish moved up the social ladder, the Jews took their place in the ring. In Britain, two of the stars of the bare-knuckle era, Daniel Mendoza and Dutch Sam, had been Jewish and the influx of Jewish refugees in the late nineteenth and early twentieth centuries produced great fighters like Ted 'Kid' Lewis and his Whitechapel acolyte Jack 'Kid' Berg, both of whom took America by storm and won world titles. At British and European title level there were Harry Mason, Matt Wells, Al Foreman, the three formidable sets of brothers Keller, Bloomfield and Brown, and the Aldgate Tiger Al Phillips.

The East End halls like Premierland, Wonderland, Mile End Arena and the Judean Club bred good fighters, and drew heavily on the local community for both participants and supporters, but over the last fifty years Jewish involvement has been mainly in promotional and managerial capacities. Only middleweight Lew Lazar and welterweight Gary Jacobs, British and European champion, have achieved any real prominence in that time.

In America, the first forty years of the century were when the Jewish fighters shone. Heavyweight champion Max Baer wore the Star of David on his shorts, but his right to do so was questioned by trainer Ray Arcel, who famously remarked 'I seen the guy in the shower. He ain't Jewish.'

JACK (KID) BERG

Probably the greatest boxing Ambassador this country ever sent to America. Relentless in fury, his colourful style of Boxing and his eager willingness to trade punches made him popular on both sides of the Atlantic. He won the British Light-weight Championship in 1934 by defeating Harry Mizler, but lost it two years later to Jimmy Walsh.

There were no such doubts about long-serving light-heavyweight champion Maxie Rosenbloom or the best of them all, Chicago's Barney Ross, who held titles at three weights between 1933 and 1938. Benny Leonard, lightweight champion from 1917 to 1925, shares legendary status with Ross, while featherweight Abe Attell reigned for nine years from 1903.

Puerto Ricans have made a disproportionate contribution to boxing history. The first world champion from the island was bantamweight Sixto Escobar in 1934, since when they can boast triple champions Wilfred Benitez and Wilfredo Vasquez, welterweight claimants Angel Espada and Felix Trinidad, and two-weights champions Carlos Ortiz and Edwin Rosario. Lightweight Esteban DeJesus was the first to beat Roberto Duran, while Hector Camacho continues to entertain more than fourteen years after winning the first of his three titles. Super-feather Sam Serrano held the WBA title between 1977 and 1983, and John-John Molina wrote his own considerable chapter in the history of that division, but super-bantam Wilfredo Gomez, who retained that title a record seventeen times before moving up to become champion at feather and super-feather, was arguably the country's number one.

MAX BAER
A German-American. Born at Omaha, Feb. 11th, 1909. He won the heavy-weight Championship of the world in 1934, by stopping Primo Carnera in eleven rounds, at Long Island City. In the following year he lost the title to James J. Braddock. He has since been knocked-out by the present world Heavy-weight Champion, Joe Louis, and during his visit to London was defeated by Tommy Farr.

The next ethnic group to make their mark on American boxing were the Latinos, best represented today by the multi-titled Oscar De La Hoya. Their successes have mainly been in the lighter divisions. Welterweight Carlos Palomino was a respected performer during his three-year tenure of the WBC welterweight title in the 1970s, at the same time that Mexican puncher Pipino Cuevas was making nine of his thirteen WBA title defences in American rings. Light-welters Zack Padilla and Carlos Gonzalez had their moments in the 1990s, while the lightweight division produced stars like Mando Ramos, Art Frias and Chango Carmona and Rodolfo Gonzalez.

Danny 'Little Red' Lopez was one of the hardest hitters in featherweight history, and Genaro Hernandez has impressed in two reigns at super-feather. Bantam Manuel Ortiz is one of the greats of that weight class, which also gave us solid champions in Richard Sandoval, Orlando and Gaby Canizales, and Albert Davila.

If the pattern is maintained, watch for a cluster of Vietnamese and Asian-Americans to dominate the game in the first decade of the new millennium.

DRAWING THE COLOUR LINE

Had the black fighters been given a fair break, it is likely that they would have ruled the sport virtually from its inception. John L. Sullivan set the standard for his successors when he announced 'I've never fought a nigger and I never will', thus obliging great fighters like Joe Jeanette, Sam McVey, Harry Wills, Sam Langford and (until 1909) Jack Johnson to waste their careers boxing each other. Langford, for example, met Wills twenty-three times, McVey fifteen, Jeanette fourteen, Jim Barry twelve and Jeff Clarke eleven. They were reduced to contesting a worthless 'Negro championship', and after Johnson's scandalous and riot-ridden spell as world champion (see *History in the Making*), no black heavyweight came close to the title until Joe Louis won it in 1937. Too often, they were forced to 'fight in handcuffs' against white prospects, and accept losses to men whom they could easily have beaten in fair competition.

Louis' success, and the unthreatening manner (to white sensibilities) in which he conducted himself paved the way for a flood of outstanding black champions in other divisions, like the immortal Sugar Ray Robinson, Archie Moore, Henry Armstrong, lightweight rivals Beau Jack, Bob Montgomery and Ike Williams, and featherweight great Sandy Saddler.

Archie Moore earned his world title the hard way, after eight years as top contender

Yet for every one who made the grade (often through selling themselves to the Mob) there were dozens of others who were denied the opportunity. Archie Moore, perhaps the greatest of all light-heavyweight champions, names middleweight contender Charlie Burley as the toughest man he ever fought, yet who remembers Burley today? Moore himself was thirty-six before he was finally given a title shot, almost eight years after becoming the leading contender. Even then, he had to box for nothing to win the title and take the short end of the purse to give defeated champion Joey Maxim – his stablemate – two thoroughly undeserved rematches before he could begin to make the title pay.

It was not until the 1960s that black fighters were finally judged on their own merits and given the chances their talent warranted. Modern boxing history is infinitely richer for that belated slice of justice.

BOXING AND THE MOB

Boxing has always attracted the slightly shadier types, but the close supervision of the sport in Britain has kept it generally free of any gangster involvement. Applications for licences in whatever capacity are rigorously vetted, and a hint of criminality is enough to guarantee rejection. In America, though, where each state is responsible for running boxing in its own territory, the Mob found it much easier to infiltrate the business. There is still no national controlling body there, and many states do not even have a Commission.

The result, in the first half of the century, was Mob involvement on a huge scale, so much so that they were even able to steer a very modestly gifted heavyweight, the Italian Primo Carnera, to the world championship in 1933. Carnera was a physical freak, the biggest man to win the title, and American gangsters quickly realised his profit potential. His European managers were squeezed out, and his new team bought, bribed and threatened a string of opponents to fall over in hick towns where their swan dives would not attract close inspection by the Commission or, more importantly, by the national press.

Unlike Moore, Primo Carnera became world champion in the easiest possible way, courtesy of the Mob

He won the title with an unconvincing knockout of Jack Sharkey, who had beaten the Italian clearly in a 'straight' fight in 1931, but after that he was thrown to the wolves and, within a year of losing the crown to Max Baer, was a penniless wreck.

His story was not unique. Many other champions benefited or suffered from Mob involvement, although a few had the nerve to stand up against them. Jack Dempsey was offered 'help' to ensure that he beat Gene Tunney in their Chicago rematch, the famous Battle of the Long Count, but declined it. Al Capone was so impressed that he sent the Dempseys a bouquet of flowers at their hotel, with a congratulatory note. (The fight, staged in Chicago on 22 September 1927, became known as the Battle of the Long Count after Dempsey, having floored Tunney in the seventh round, refused to heed the recently-introduced rule and go to a neutral corner until Tunney had risen. Referee Dave Barry, quite correctly, did not commence the count until Dempsey had finally obeyed his command, by which time Tunney had already been down for five seconds. When the champion got up at nine, he had actually been on the floor for fourteen seconds.)

Others took what help they could get. Bantamweight champion Charley Phil Rosenberg's reign was dogged by controversy, including a 1925 episode when he was suspended indefinitely and his opponent Eddie Shea banned for life after Shea had taken a dive in the fourth, allegedly under threat of death. Bat Battalino, a featherweight contemporary of Rosenberg's, lost his title by arrangement to his stablemate Freddie Miller in 1931. His account of the affair is memorable. 'I stretched out', he recalled. 'The referee says for me to get up. I told him to count.'

Mob involvement reached its zenith in the 1940s and 1950s, when a pair of unsavoury characters called Blinky Palermo and Frankie Carbo controlled the destiny of titles. They were undercover managers of most of the champions and leading contenders, and through their manipulation of the then all-powerful International Boxing Club (IBC), which enjoyed a near-monopoly on world title shows, they controlled the promotional side as well. They said who won and who lost, and time and again engineered a series of fights involving the same two men, both under their control, thus tying up championships for years.

The quickest way to a title fight was to deal with them, as Jake La Motta found when he was rewarded with a middleweight title shot after throwing a fight to the Mob-run light-heavyweight Billy Fox in 1947. They kept trouble-makers in line through the Boxing Guild, an alliance of managers who ensured that any boxer attempting to leave his manager would be blackballed and denied work. It happened to the great lightweight Ike Williams, who was frozen out until he signed with Palermo and was promptly rewarded with a title chance.

Their power was finally broken in 1960 by the Kefauver Commission, a US Senate body which was set up to investigate organised crime. The IBC was disbanded, as was the Boxing Guild, and although it would be naive to claim that the bad guys have gone away altogether, at least their activities in the modern game are considerably harder to detect.

EARLY STARTERS

Only three men have contested a world title in their first fight, and unsurprisingly they all lost. Jack Skelly was knocked out in eight rounds by George Dixon for the featherweight title in New Orleans on 6 September 1892, Pete Rademacher went out in six against Floyd Patterson for the heavyweight championship in Seattle on 22 August 1957, and light-fly Rafael Lovera was knocked out in four by Luis Estaba for the vacant WBC belt on 13 September 1975.

Saensak Muangsurin of Thailand was the quickest winner, taking the WBC light-welterweight title in his third Western-style bout: however, he had considerable experience as a Thai boxer before that. Leon Spinks had only had seven fights when he took the heavyweight tile from Muhammad Ali, while Scottish light-flyweight Paul Weir lifted the WBO title in his sixth fight.

LOSING COUNT

The highest number of counts taken in a fight is forty-six, in the 1909 battle in Paris between Joe Jeanette and Sam McVey. Jeanette was floored twenty-seven times to McVey's nineteen, but still managed to win when McVey collapsed at the start of the forty-ninth round.

British bantamweight Danny O'Sullivan set a lasting record when he was knocked down fourteen times in a world title challenge against Vic Toweel in Johannesburg on 2 December 1950. O'Sullivan took eight counts in the fifth round, but survived until the tenth, when he retired.

HARD GRAFT

The highest verifiable number of fights recorded by any professional is Englishman's Len Wickwar's 466 between 1928 and 1947. Americans Jack Britton (342 between 1905–30) and Johnny Dundee (337 between 1910–32) are next, and Chelsea welterweight Billy Bird is fourth with 321 between 1920 and 1948. Bird also features on the list of those scoring the most inside the distance wins. His total of 125 earns him third place behind Young Stribling (126 between 1921–33) and former light-heavyweight champion Archie Moore, who tops the table with 145 between 1936–63.

The longest winning streak was 183, compiled by Gloucester lightweight Hal Bagwell between 1938–48 – yet Bagwell never even fought for a British title.

TIPPING THE SCALES

1930s heavyweight champion Primo Carnera, at 270 lbs, was the heaviest ever to fight for a title when he defended against former light-heavyweight champion Tommy Loughran at Miami on 1 March 1934. That fight also saw the biggest discrepancy between opponents' weights, as Loughran, 184 lbs, conceded a staggering 86 lbs – 6 st 12 lbs. He still managed to last the full fifteen rounds.

Carnera took part in the fight with the greatest aggregate weight, 488 3/4 lbs, when, weighing 259 1/2 lbs, he outpointed Paolino Uzcudun (229 1/4 lbs) in Rome on 22 October 1933. This was also the only time that the undisputed world heavyweight title was contested by two Europeans: Carnera was Italian, Uzcudun a Basque.

WHO'S WHO IN THE ALPHABET WORLD

IBB	–	International Boxing Board
IBC	–	International (formerly Intercontinental) Boxing Council
IBF	–	International Boxing Federation
IBO	–	International Boxing Organisation
WAA	–	World Athletic Association
WBA	–	World Boxing Association
WBB	–	World Boxing Board
WBC	–	World Boxing Council
WBC	–	World Boxing Commission
WBF	–	World Boxing Federation
WBO	–	World Boxing Organisation
WBU	–	World Boxing Union

PLAYING THE NAME GAME

How would you like to have your very own world boxing governing body? It's simple: all you need is a set of initials which haven't been used before (but be quick – the possible combinations are being snapped up fast). Then print your letterheading, invest in a few tasteful plastic championship belts, announce your organisation's existence in the trade press, and wait for the sanction fees to roll in. It helps to get your outfit up and running, of course, if you have a tame promoter who's prepared to stage a few of your title fights. Better still, find a former champion who is between 'legitimate' titles at the moment and install him as your 'world champion'. No matter how high-profile he is, no boxer is likely to turn down a free championship belt, and even if he dumps yours in the nearest dustbin as soon as he gets a crack at a more established title, you will still have had value and publicity from his tenure of your title.

If any of the above sounds implausible to the casual fan, be assured that it has all happened already. Of the twelve (at last count) organisations currently cluttering the scene, only four were established by combinations of existing administrative bodies such as national or regional commissions. All the others were invented by private individuals, who in most cases had a background in boxing administration or promotion, and they were usually able to find a big-name fighter prepared to accept recognition as their champion.

The World Boxing Union (WBU), for example, was launched by Jon Robinson from his home in a Norfolk village, and attracted instant attention by bestowing its heavyweight belt on George Foreman, who was in dispute with the IBF and WBA at the time. The IBC (International Boxing Council), first called the Intercontinental Boxing Council, was established in 1990 by an eccentric 94-year-old manager called Marty Cohen, who was looking after Hector 'Macho' Camacho and needed a world title of any sort for him. Since none of the legitimate titles was available, Cohen simply created his own, and immediately set new standards in administrative incompetence by authorising two fights for the IBC heavyweight title on the same night, on different coasts. Cohen has since died, but the organisation, now run by Joseph 'Blackie' Genaro, survives at a very low level of recognition. It is significant only because it was the first of the bodies to be set up by an individual, rather than a group of commissions.

POWER OF THE PRESS

For the first sixty years of the century, boxing jogged along fairly comfortably without any world governing body, legitimate or otherwise. It was very much an American-centred sport, and since most of the big fights took place in New York, the New York State Athletic Commission became the single most powerful administrative body in the world. Their only potential rival was the National Boxing Association (NBA), which came into being when an Englishman, William A. Gavin, called a meeting of thirteen state commissions – held, ironically, in New York City in 1920. Gavin had not actually wanted to establish a governing body at all: his plan was to set up an International Sporting Club on the lines of the London-based National Sporting Club, a dinner-boxing club for the affluent which doubled as the *de facto* ruler of the sport in Britain. Gavin's project was side-lined and instead the NBA became an administrative body, installing and deposing champions and issuing rankings lists.

From time to time world titles would fall into dispute, and when that happened the various commissions around the world lined up behind either New York or the NBA. The NY faction included the European Boxing Union and the British Boxing Board of Control, which had finally replaced the NSC in 1929, and contained the nucleus of the grouping which, in 1963, would form the World Boxing Council.

Generally, though, the sporting public were content to accept the word of Nat Fleischer and his monthly *Ring* magazine as the ultimate authority, which from a 1990s perspective seems an extraordinary degree of trust and power to repose with one man. But then there was nothing new about the media's ability to influence events in boxing. In bare-knuckle Britain, Pierce Egan's *Boxiana* and, later,

Henry Downes Miles' *Pugilistica* ruled on the merits of rival claimants, while in America, in the last quarter of the nineteenth century, as prize-fighting grew in popularity there, Richard Kyle Fox's *Police Gazette* fulfilled the same function. Fox was a Dubliner who emigrated to America in 1871 when he was twenty-nine, and within two years he had saved half of the $400 needed to buy a discredited and failing scandal sheet called the *National Police Gazette*.

Fox proved a publishing genius with a flair for imaginative sales gimmicks, designed to boost public awareness of his 10-cent product. In addition to giving away more than $250,000 in cash prizes, he awarded a whole range of belts, trophies and cups commemorating the most bizarre and obscure achievements of the type which today are chronicled in the *Guinness Book of Records*. But his real achievement was to recognise the public's craving for sports news. He introduced a full sports section, and circulation surged. Prize-fighting was still illegal in all the (then) thirty-eight states of America, but reporting it was not and Fox concentrated his coverage on fights and races. It was so successful that there was even a British edition, which was launched in 1896. In the same year he published the first of his annual record books, which continued until a fire in 1918 destroyed the paper's offices and all its records.

The foundation of *Ring* magazine four years later marked the start of the *Gazette*'s decline, although it struggled on until 1932. The *Ring*'s policy of recording the result of every fight, however obscure, in tiny type at the back of the magazine quickly established its authority with the serious fan, and the monthly ratings Fleischer introduced soon became enormously influential, to the point where it would be virtually impossible for a man to get a title fight if he was not in the magazine's top ten.

The situation changed dramatically in the early 1960s, when the TV boom in boxing began and the Las Vegas casino money started to attract the big fights away from New York. The power of the New York Commission evaporated overnight, and a vacuum was created. It was soon filled, as the major promoters (each of whom usually worked exclusively with a particular TV company) recognised the need for more championships to keep their TV paymasters happy. With only one, or occasionally two, world champions in each of the eight categories, there simply weren't enough to go around.

The solution was two-fold: first, encourage the creation of 'world governing bodies', and second, expand the number of weight classes from the classic eight (fly, bantam, feather, light, welter, middle, light-heavy and heavy) to the present seventeen.

There was some justification on safety grounds for expanding the categories, since the gaps between the original eight were far too wide and often resulted in dangerous mismatches, but many of the new divisions in the lighter weight categories reflect commercial pressure from the expanding Oriental market, where fighters over 10 st are rare.

Although the poundage for the new divisions is uniform amongst all the controlling bodies, they have never been able to agree on what they should be called, thus providing a further source of confusion for the casual fan. Is it cruiser or junior-heavy (190 lbs); light-middle, junior-middle or super-welter (154 lbs); light-welter, junior-welter or super-light (140 lbs); super-feather or junior light (130 lbs); super-bantam or junior-feather (122 lbs); super-fly or junior-bantam (115 lbs); light-fly or mini-flyweight (108 lbs)?

The organisations multiplied almost as quickly as the weight categories. There had been a serious attempt to establish a genuine world governing body in 1957, when a World Championships Committee was established consisting of members from the NBA, the NY Commission, the EBU and the BBBC, but it fell apart in 1959 when the NBA broke ranks to strip Sugar Ray Robinson of his title because of his reluctance to defend against Carmen Basilio and installed its own middleweight champion, Gene Fullmer.

THE ALPHABET BOYS ARRIVE

Three years later, the NBA re-named itself the World Boxing Association, although its officers remained either American or Canadian for the next twelve years. The new body consisted of fifty-one state commissions and a handful of national governing bodies, but was so American-biased that it could never hope to be a truly international organisation. Any single American state – even one in which there was little or no boxing – had one vote, exactly the same as entire countries like Britain or Mexico. Inevitably, the non-Americans split from the WBA at the 1963 convention and formed their own group, the World Boxing Council (WBC). Sixteen countries were founder members, and the new body subdivided into seven regional federations, one of which was North America. Since the United States had to share North America's voting rights with Mexico and Canada, there was no possibility of the WBC becoming American dominated.

But even if they couldn't control the WBC administratively, American dollars ensured that their interests were not neglected. Don King, who emerged as a major promoter in the early 1970s, cultivated a close relationship with the WBC's President Jose Sulaiman of Mexico. King became the WBC's biggest backer, promoting more of their title fights than any of his rivals and, through the sanction fees the WBC demanded for every championship promotion, being the largest contributor to their exchequer. In return, the WBC obliged him whenever they could by favouring King's fighters in the rankings or rubber-stamping title fights of dubious quality.

Don King

The WBA proved even more malleable, this time in favour of King's chief rival Bob Arum. In 1974 a Panamanian-led coup ousted the old WBA leadership, and the organisation has remained in Latin hands ever since. It quickly earned such a reputation for corruption that it became known in the trade as the World Bribes Association, a reputation enhanced by a series of revealing interviews Arum gave to *Ring* magazine and *Sports Illustrated* in which he catalogued payment of bribes through a Puerto Rican 'bag man' called Pepe Cordero, who held no office in the WBA but later founded the WBO.

Arum's disenchantment with the WBA, and America's lack of administrative power in the organisation, led to an attempted coup (headed by Bobby Lee) at the 1982 convention. When the coup failed, the rebels walked out of the convention and announced the formation of their own organisation, the International Boxing Federation, under Lee's presidency. The IBF's constitution required that its President must be American, but even so they gained widespread support from the Orient, particularly the rapidly-expanding Korean market and the Philippines. American promoters like the powerful Main Events group worked with them in preference to their Latin-led rivals, as did Arum, and they also made inroads in Europe.

In 1988 Cordero, backed by a few dissident commissions, left the WBA and launched the World Boxing Organisation, which, although it had an American president in Ed Levine, was totally owned by the Cordero family. Barry Hearn helped establish it in Britain, mainly through Chris Eubank's high-profile fights, and when Cordero died in 1995 and the WBO reorganised, Frank Warren became their busiest and most successful promoter.

The International Boxing Organisation (IBO) followed in 1992, and the World Boxing Federation emerged in 1993. Britain's representative, the World Boxing Union (WBU), was launched in 1994 by Jon Robinson, previously the IBF's European chief.

The last of the 1990s newcomers was the International Boxing Association, which broke away from the IBC and is run by former IBC vice-president, Dean Chance. There are a few others far out on the lunatic fringe, like the World Boxing Commission (which sanctioned one title fight in 1997 and then disappeared) and the World Athletic Association, a reorganised version of a body which first appeared in 1981 as a vehicle for Sean O'Grady, who had just been stripped of his WBA lightweight title. His father Pat founded the WAA, naming Sean as lightweight champion and his son-in-law Monte Masters as heavyweight champion. Sean lost his title in his first defence, and Monte (whom Pat's daughter subsequently divorced) was booted off his throne, presumably for marital misdemeanours. In the crazy world of the Alphabet Boys, nothing surprises.

RATING THE ALPHABET BOYS

1. World Boxing Council

Despite its uncomfortably close relationship with Don King, the WBC is the most effective and representative of the would-be governing bodies. It has a wider geographical range of members than any of its rivals, and although the presidency appears to be Jose Sulaiman's for life, other nationalities are well represented at all levels in the organisation. Under Sulaiman, the WBC has done much good work in improving safety in the sport, funding extensive medical research programmes. They were responsible for reducing championship fights from fifteen rounds to twelve, instituted a rigorous and successful drug-testing scheme, and have also introduced adequate insurance cover for boxers competing in WBC fights.

WBC titles are generally regarded as the most prestigious, and their current list of champions includes outstanding performers like Lennox Lewis, Oscar De La Hoya and Ricardo Lopez, the Mexican straw-weight with the best record in boxing.

2. World Boxing Association

The WBA has broadened its membership base and

TOTAL NUMBER OF CHAMPIONSHIP FIGHTS STAGED BY EACH OF THE FOUR MAJOR GOVERNING BODIES IN THE 1990s (until 6.6.98)	
WBC	
heavies	17
cruisers	15
light-heavies	14
super-middles	20
middles	15
light-middles	24
welters	18
light-welters	19
lights	22
super-feathers	16
feathers	21
super-bantams	24
bantams	26
super-flies	22
flyweights	21
light-flies	26
straws	23
TOTALS	**343**

has shed the shady image it had in the 1970s, mainly as a result of the strong South African influence which emerged when the WBA, alone amongst the governing bodies, admitted South Africa to membership during the apartheid era. Their decision was swayed by the vast revenue being generated by the Sun City gambling resort, which soon became a major championship venue, but the South African officials, notably Mike Mortimer and Stanley Christodolou, were men of the highest probity who curbed the worst of the WBA's financial excesses. The WBA's titles remain amongst the sport's most prestigious, and as only four of their championships are currently held by Americans, they can claim to be a truly international organisation. In Ghanaian welterweight Ike Quartey and Russian lightweight Orzoubak Nazarov, they have impressive standard-bearers.

3. The International Boxing Federation

The IBF's American bias is plain from the fact that eleven of its champions are US citizens while another, Canadian Arturo Gatti, does all his fighting in America. They tried to expand into Europe, setting up their own IBF–Europe championships as a rival to the European Boxing Union's titles, but failed to attract any support. An attempt to set up IBF–UK, to compete with the British Board of Control, was equally unsuccessful, and their efforts now are mainly concentrated in America and the Orient. But they have many high-profile champions like Evander Holyfield, Bernard Hopkins and Johnny Tapia, and have also gained a useful foothold in South Africa, home of two of their champions.

WBA	
heavies	18
cruisers	17
light-heavies	18
super-middles	20
middles	20
light-middles	19
welters	16
light-welters	21
lights	17
super-feathers	21
feathers	22
super-bantams	26
bantams	19
super-flies	24
flyweights	25
light-flies	21
straws	25
TOTALS	**349**

Naseem Hamed ... his
potential remains awesome

4. The World Boxing Organisation

The WBO was seen as something of a joke when it first emerged in 1988 under the dubious guidance of the WBA's former bribes collector Pepe Cordero, but a complete change of management since Cordero's death has given it credibility. Its status has been greatly enhanced by champions of the quality of Oscar De La Hoya, Naseem Hamed and Darius Michalczewski, each of whom relinquished rival versions of the title in favour of keeping their WBO belts. Eleven countries are currently represented in their list of champions.

5. The World Boxing Union

A well-run and ambitious outfit, the WBU has made rapid strides in its short history and is particularly successful in Thailand. It also boasts a wide geographical spread, with three champions each from South Africa, America and Italy. It has attracted some big-name champions like George Foreman, Corrie Sanders, Angel Manfredy, Kevin Kelley and Frank Tate. Its main flaw is an ultra-relaxed championship policy which allows any two men ranked in the top 100 by the Bristol-based International World Boxing Rankings to contest their titles.

6. The International Boxing Organisation

This Chicago-based body has made only tentative moves to expand outside America: three of its champions are from Denmark, where the local promoter Mogens Palle makes it a policy to work with any organisation, however obscure (he also manages an IBC champion, Soren Sondergaard, and a WBF titlist, Frederic Alvarez). But it has

IBF	
heavies	18
cruisers	15
light-heavies	19
super-middles	20
middles	20
light-middles	22
welters	16
light-welters	21
lights	23
super-feathers	21
feathers	24
super-bantams	23
bantams	24
super-flies	24
flyweights	19
light-flies	25
straws	31
TOTALS	**365**

recently acquired a persuasive and experienced president in American lawyer Ed Levine, the former president of both the WBO and WBU, and could improve its status under his leadership.

7. The World Boxing Federation

The WBF's power-base is in the Orient. Five of its champions are Thais, with one each from Japan, Indonesia and the Philippines. They also boast champions from America, Australia, Sweden and Mexico, so have a reasonably strong international flavour. The WBF can claim the best, and most elaborately-named, champion of any of the 'Second Division' bodies: Thai super-flyweight Samson Dutch Boy Gym, who started life as Samson Lukchaopormasak and later became Samson Elite Gym. (In Thailand, boxers adopt the names of their gyms, which are operated by their sponsors.)

8. The International Boxing Council

The IBC can now claim some decent champions, notably heavyweight Michael Grant, a threat to any of the 'genuine' title-holders. Three other current IBC representatives, Robert Daniels, Steve Little and Hector Camacho, have held legitimate titles in their prime, but with ten IBC titles vacant at the time of writing, their future looks unpromising.

9. The International Boxing Association

Like their parent body, the IBC, the IBA presently have ten vacancies on their list of champions, which does not augur well for their future. They have two outstanding champions in South African light-flyweight Jake Matlala, who formerly held

WBO	
heavies	13
cruisers	19
light-heavies	20
super-middles	27
middles	21
light-middles	16
welters	18
light-welters	22
lights	18
super-feathers	18
feathers	26
super-bantams	20
bantams	16
super-flies	21
flyweights	21
light-flies	12
straws	12
TOTALS	**320**

WBO titles at light-fly and flyweight, and featherweight Orlando Canizales, who made a record sixteen defences of the IBF bantamweight title. Their light-middleweight champion, Bronco McKart, is also a former WBO titlist at the weight.

10. The Rest

Beyond comment.

IS THERE A SOLUTION?

So long as there is a TV slot to fill, and commercial breaks to sell, there will always be a promoter with a 'world championship' to offer and a TV company willing to buy it from him regardless of the fight's legitimacy as a title contest. The great mass of TV viewers do not understand the near-anarchy in which boxing exists, and are incapable of assessing the relative merits of a dozen or more rival claimants for the same world championship. They are happy just to settle down with their six-pack and watch the boxing, on the premise that if it's billed as a world title fight, looks like a world title fight and the winner gets a world title belt, then it's a world title fight.

Most people in the trade take the same pragmatic view as that held by Mogens Palle, the promoter who enjoys a monopoly on the sport in Denmark. 'The fans couldn't care less what label a fight carries, so long as it's a good fight', he says, and he practises what he preaches, as, over his forty years in the business, he has promoted title fights featuring WBC, WBA, WBO, WBF, IBO and IBC titles.

The flood of organisations seems unstoppable. They

TOTAL	
heavies	66
cruisers	66
light-heavies	71
super-middles	87
middles	76
light-middles	81
welters	68
light-welters	83
lights	80
super-feathers	76
feathers	93
super-bantams	93
bantams	85
super-flies	91
flyweights	86
light-flies	84
straws	91
TOTALS	**1377**

do not require any official permission to exist, since boxing is not subject to any form of government control, and as most of the minor organisations are run purely as private profit-making commercial ventures there is little chance that they will ever cease operations in the wider interests of the sport. There is growing pressure in America to bring boxing under federal control, which, if it comes about, could seriously weaken the position of all the competing bodies, and especially those like the WBC and WBA which trade in North America but are based outside the country.

But in the absence of government controls, the only hope of restoring some degree of sanity is for the major TV outlets to operate a quality control system and refuse to screen so-called title fights which do not involve the best men at the weight. It is rare for any American company to show title fights involving any of the minor organisations, unless featuring a boxer whose reputation is bigger than the organisation for whose title he is competing, like Hector Camacho and the IBC or James Toney and the IBO. It does not seem such a giant step to apply the same policy to the four major governing bodies, but financial interests are so deeply entrenched that it is unlikely to happen.

The TV stations are in the hands of their contracted promoters, and will screen whatever they offer them. In Britain, for example, Sky Sports feature all Frank Warren's many WBO title fights – at the beginning of 1998 he had seven WBO champions on his books – but in the unlikely event of Warren switching his allegiance to the WBU or the IBO, Sky would no doubt trust his judgement and throw their weight – and their chequebook – behind that body.

So the outlook is bleak for the purists and the traditionalists, although they can at least console themselves with the reflection that, however many championships there may be, sooner or later the real champions emerge. Not even his rival title-holder could dispute Naseem Hamed's claim to be the world's best featherweight, or argue that Ricardo Lopez is not the game's outstanding straw-weight. Quality tells, in the end.

BRITAIN AND EUROPE

The sport in Britain was run by the autocratic, self-appointed National Sporting Club until 1929 (see *History* chapter – *Early Days In Britain*), when it was supplanted by the British Boxing Board of Control. The NSC was originally granted a permanent seat on the new Board, but had to relinquish that in 1936 when the Club set up as a commercial promoter in its own right.

The Board is sub-divided into eight area councils, most of which contain representatives from local licence-holders in various capacities, including boxers, managers and promoters. The Administrative Stewards, Championship Committee and Stewards of Appeal are mostly men with no direct financial interest in the business, with the legal profession being heavily represented. Membership is by invitation rather than election, but despite its undemocratic nature, the system works well and the Board's efficiency and reputation make it a role model for national controlling bodies world-wide.

The Board is responsible for every aspect of boxing, including licensing all participants, supervising tournaments, setting medical standards, controlling championships and adjudicating on disputes between licence-holders. It is funded by licence fees and by taxes on promotions and TV revenue. It was a founder member of the European Boxing Union, the WBC and the Commonwealth Championships Council, which controls the sport in British Commonwealth countries, and has taken a leading role in them all.

The first attempt to control boxing in Europe came in 1911 when a French boxing writer, Victor Breyer, tried to involve the NSC in a new organisation he was setting up, the International Boxing Union, to administer European championships. The Club refused to become a member of any other body, but Breyer went ahead anyway with backing from Switzerland and France, which was then a major power in world boxing. The IBU instituted its own world titles, which were contested up to the outbreak of the First World War in 1914.

The IBU reappeared between the wars, principally to advance the claims of worthy European contenders like Marcel Thil, Valentin Angelmann, Maurice Holtzer and Gustav Roth, who were being frozen out by the more powerful American interests. At a convention in Rome in May 1938, the delegates agreed to withdraw recognition from their own champions, to facilitate the reunification of the titles. Their championships had never been more than a glorified European title, since only three of their title fights took place outside Europe. The IBU was then overtaken by the Second World War in 1939, and its successor, the European Boxing Union, was not formed until 1948.

The EBU, which claims the affiliation of every

European country in which boxing is staged, is one of the most important and influential federations in the world. It was dominated by the Italians for many years, under the dictatorial reign of its General Secretary Piero Pini, who tended to run it as his personal fiefdom. Since Pini's death, however, it has become a model of efficiency and impartiality. The EBU issues its own monthly ratings, which are compiled by consultation amongst the member countries, and titles can only be contested by rated boxers. The spread of professional boxing throughout what used to be the Communist bloc in Eastern Europe has strengthened the EBU greatly.

The average layman probably believes that boxing is still governed by the rules which bear the Marquess of Queensberry's name. But that worthy had nothing to do with drawing up 'his' rules: they were the work of John Graham Chambers of the London Athletic Club, who, in the slavish fashion of the day, sought to lend his ideas some respectability by attracting aristocratic sponsorship. Queensberry would certainly be hopelessly at sea in the world of modern professional boxing, with its 'technical decisions', no-foul rule, and the plethora of complicated refinements to what was once a simple code of practice, designed to bring some order to an increasingly chaotic sport.

Bare-knuckle fighting used to be conducted with the minimum of regulation. Practically everything was permissible, from gouging to stamping, kicking or throwing. Note that the old engravings of bare-knucklers never show a man with long, flowing locks or a bushy moustache, even though both would have been considered the height of fashion in the first half of the eighteenth century. It was considered perfectly acceptable to grab an opponent by the hair or moustache, so the fighters invariably took the obvious precaution before a battle.

About the only rule that was enforced was that which deemed a round to have ended when one man went down, even though that was easily abused by unscrupulous fighters who would drop to their knees at the first hint of trouble. They did not have to worry about points decisions going against them, since all fights were to the finish.

John Broughton, the champion of England, drew up his own set of rules in 1743 in reaction to the death of one of his opponents, George Stevenson. They were short and uncomplicated: complete with eccentric punctuation and capitals, they read:

1 – That a square of a Yard be chalked in the middle of the Stage, and in each fresh set-to after a fall, or being from the rails, each second is to bring his Man to the side of the Square and place him opposite to the other, and until they are fairly set-to at the Lines, it shall not be lawful for one to strike at the other.

2 – That, in order to prevent any Disputes, the time a man lies after a fall if the Second does not bring his Man to the side of the square within the space of half a minute, he shall be deemed a beaten Man.

3 – That in every Main Battle no person whatever shall be upon the Stage, except the Principals and their Seconds, the same rule to be observed in Bye-battles, except that in the latter Mr. Broughton is allowed to be upon the Stage to keep decorum and to assist Gentlemen in getting to their places, provided always he does not interfere in the Battle; and whoever pretends to infringe these Rules to be turned immediately out of the house. Everybody is to quit the Stage as soon as the Champions are stripped, before the set-to.

4 – That no Champion be deemed beaten, unless he fails coming up to the line in the limited time or that his own Second declares him beaten. No Second is to be allowed to ask his Man's adversary any questions or advise him to give out.

5 – That in Bye-battles the winning man have two-thirds of the Money given, which shall be publicly

JOHN BROUGHTON
Born in 1704, he can be termed the "Father of Boxing." He was the first real Champion of England, and made boxing a science. The first rules of what was called the "True Art of Boxing," were formed and set up by him. He fought many battles with varying success until 1750, when he was beaten by Jack Slack. He was then in his forty-sixth year. He died in 1789.

divided upon the Stage, notwithstanding private agreements to the contrary.

6 – That, to prevent Disputes, in every Main Battle the Principals shall, upon coming to the Stage, choose from among the Gentlemen present two Umpires, who shall absolutely decide all Disputes that may arise about the Battle; and if the two Umpires cannot agree, the said Umpires to choose a third, who is to determine it.

7 – That no person is to hit his Adversary when he is down or seize him by the ham, the breeches, or any part below the waist; a man on his knees to be reckoned down.

Broughton's Rules were superseded in 1838 by the London Prize Rules (which were revised in 1853 and again in 1866). These provided for a 24ft square ring, bounded with ropes. When a man was floored or thrown (wrestling was still an integral part of the developing sport) the round ended and the fighter was helped to his corner, being allowed a full thirty seconds to recover and a further eight seconds to 'come up to scratch', which was a line scratched in the turf of the ring floor. Kicking, butting, biting and low blows were declared fouls, as was the previously-common practice of going down without being hit, automatically finishing the round.

The Queensberry Rules, drawn up in 1867 for the control initially of amateur boxing, differed in four main respects: contestants must wear padded gloves, rounds would be of three minutes duration with a minute's interval, wrestling throws would not be permitted, and a floored boxer had to rise within ten seconds or be declared the loser. For a

JEM MACE
Born in 1831, was a Norfolk man. He was of medium build with a well-developed body and had black hair and dark eyes, and was known at one time as "The Swaffham Gipsy," though he claimed English parentage. He became Champion of England. He was also a musician and could play the fiddle extremely well. He died in 1910, at the age of 79.

while the two sets of rules co-existed, but as boxing techniques developed, the Queensberry Rules became the more popular.

The introduction of Queensberry Rules saw the end of the classic bare-knuckle 'squaring up' stance. In bare-knuckle fighting, the elbows and forearms were part of the defensive armoury, but now that gloves could be used for the same purpose, the modern stance evolved.

Jem Mace, one of the last great bare-knuckle champions, won his title under London Rules in 1861, but greatly preferred Queensberry's version and became a powerful advocate for their adoption around the world. He travelled extensively in America (which was rapidly overtaking England as the home of prize-fighting), Australia and New Zealand, where his best-known protégé was Bob Fitzsimmons.

It was John L. Sullivan, one of Mace's successors as prize ring champion, who ensured the ultimate victory of Queensberry over London Rules. Prize-fighting was illegal and organisers and participants alike ran the very real risk of arrest and fine or imprisonment. He had won his title under London Rules, but when he was fined $500 for defending against Jake Kilrain (who got two months on an assault-and-battery charge), Sullivan had had enough.

'In all the fights I have been in under the London Prize Ring Rules I have not only lost money but have also had the care and worriment incidental to arrests, trials and penalties', he announced. 'It has always cost me more money to get out of my fights under those rules than I have ever gained by them.

JOHN L. SULLIVAN
Born in U.S.A. in 1858. Became Champion of the World. He was just under 6ft. in height and weighed about 14 stone. He was an extremely well-built and powerful fighter, and depended on his strength, rather than on science. He was a very popular champion, particularly in America. He died in 1918, at the age of 60.

Again, I have never seen a fight under the London
Prize Ring Rules but what those present were of a
rougher character than I have ever seen under
Marquess of Queensberry Rules, and wherever the
rowdy element predominates there is always sure
to be trouble.'

When he issued his famous challenge to Frank
Slavin, Charlie Mitchell and James J.
Corbett in
1891, it stipulated that 'The Marquess of
Queensberry Rules must govern this contest, as I
want fighting, not foot racing.' That announcement
marked the death of the prize ring era, and the
birth of the game as we know it today.

There was no smooth and seamless handover,
however. As boxing became organised around the
world, each local commission or controlling body
adopted their own variation on the Queensberry
Rules, so that the position eventually became
incredibly complicated. In many parts of America
during the first twenty years of this century, boxing
to a decision was illegal, as a consequence of the
Frawley Law. This became known as the No
Decision era, when bets on the outcome of a
particular fight would be settled on the basis of
the opinion of a mutually agreed ringside reporter
(a 'newspaper verdict').

Titles could only change hands on a knockout or
stoppage, provided both men were inside the
division's weight limit – and those limits fluctuated
wildly, often being set arbitrarily by the champion
as the poundage he could reach with the least effort.
The No Decision era was a gift for strong-chinned
champions like featherweight Johnny Kilbane,
who won the title in 1912 and was able to hide
behind the rule until 1923, when he was finally

BOB FITZSIMMONS
A Champion of the World.
Born at Helston, Cornwall,
June 4th, 1862. He saw
much of the World as a
young man, eventually
becoming an American
citizen. He stood 5ft.
11¾ins. and weighed only
11 stone 4lb. His chest
measurement was 44ins.,
and his arms and shoulders
were those of a giant. He
was never a great boxer,
but vastly wise in experience, and ring-craft was
his forte. Died Oct., 1917.

MILLION-DOLLAR MARK

Jack Dempsey's heavyweight title defence against French war hero Georges Carpentier at Boyle's Thirty Acres, Jersey City, on 2 July 1921 was the first promotion to draw over $1m at the gate. A crowd of 80,000 paid $1,789,238, of which Dempsey was guaranteed $300,000. A record 700 journalists from around the world covered the fight, which was also the first title fight to be broadcast.

MARATHON MEN

Mike McTigue from Co. Clare holds the distinction of winning the last world title bout to go more than fifteen rounds. He took the world light-heavyweight title from Battling Siki in Dublin on, appropriately, St Patrick's Day 1923. The last scheduled twenty-rounds world title fight took place sixteen years later, when Joe Louis knocked out Bob Pastor in the eleventh round.

IN THE PICTURE

Len Harvey's points win over Jock McAvoy for the British light-heavyweight title on 4 April 1938 was the first to be shown on TV. Five years earlier, on 22 August 1933, Archie Sexton and Laurie Raiteri boxed a televised exhibition match at Broadcasting House, London.

TRIPLE HITTER

Only one man, Henry Armstrong, has ever held three world titles simultaneously. He completed his unique hat-trick by outpointing Lou Ambers on 17 August 1938 to add the lightweight title to his featherweight and welterweight championships, across a weight span of 21 lbs. Modern regulations bar boxers from holding titles in more than one division at the same time, so Armstrong's place in the record book is assured.

PERFECT SCORE

Heavyweight champion Rocky Marciano retired on 27 April 1956 with a perfect record of forty-nine fights and forty-nine wins, of which only six went the distance. He remains the only heavyweight champion to go through his entire career without a single defeat.

Only two other champions remain undefeated, bantamweight Jimmy Barry (1891–99) and lightweight Jack McAuliffe (1885–97).

REVENGE IS SWEET

Floyd Patterson, already a history-maker as the youngest heavyweight champion, became the first to regain the title when he knocked out Ingemar Johansson in five rounds on 20 June 1960. The Swede had humiliated him in three rounds a year previously. Patterson claimed yet another first on 22 July 1963 when he and Sonny Liston became the first to earn over $1m when they each got $1,434,000 for their heavyweight title rematch. The money was some consolation for Patterson who, for the second time, was flattened by Liston in the opening round.

BELTED UP

Ever-popular heavyweight Henry Cooper is the only British boxer to win three Lonsdale Belts outright, a feat he accomplished by stopping Billy Walker in six rounds at Wembley on 6 November 1967. Board rules now prevent any boxer from winning more than one Belt outright. (In order to win a Belt outright, a boxer had to win three title contests at the same weight.)

knocked out. During that eleven-year reign he fought sixty-three times under the No Decision rule, losing nine 'newspaper verdicts' and boxing five draws.

When New York finally repealed the Frawley Law in 1920 and legalised decisions, the rest of the American states quickly followed suit, since New York was the most active fight centre in the country.

Other areas of confusion emerged, including the No Foul rule, operated in most American states, which held that a fighter could not win by disqualification. It was introduced as a consequence of the antics of British heavyweight Phil Scott, known derisively as Phaintin' Phil, who claimed disqualification victories in several important championship eliminators in the late 1920s. Britain rigorously opposed the rule, on the grounds that it was a direct encouragement of bad sportsmanship; that continues to be its attitude today.

Britain has always maintained a stubborn independence of thought, sometimes past the point of logic. For years it continued to score using a complicated system of fractions, awarding the winner of a round five points and the loser either 4 3/4 or 4 1/2. Britain was, until recently, just about the only country in the world not to operate a mandatory eight count, which was a frequent source of bewilderment to visiting boxers, who still wonder why we persist in allowing the referee sole and absolute responsibility for determining the outcome when virtually every other jurisdiction uses either three judges and a non-scoring referee or two judges and a scoring referee.

Britain has also consistently opposed the three-knockdown rule favoured by New York, under which three knockdowns in any one round means an automatic stoppage, or the 'accidental butt' rule, which provides for a points decision to be rendered if, because of an accidental clash of heads, one man is too badly cut to continue.

The biggest area of confusion, which heightened almost every year during the 1990s, as new would-be 'governing bodies' emerged, were the rules governing world title fights. The disputes became near-insurmountable when more than one governing body was involved, and the rules meetings – interminable conferences on the evening before the fight, designed to agree a mutually acceptable set of regulations – became a feature of world championship shows.

Finally, in October 1997 at a meeting in Atlantic City, the Presidents of four of the major organisations – the WBC, IBF, WBO and WBU – came up with a compromise set of rules to control championship fights in America. The major points agreed were:

(a) no three knockdown rule
(b) a boxer is given a 10 count if he falls onto the ring apron, but is allowed 20 seconds to re-enter the ring if he falls off it or onto another surface, such as a press table
(c) a boxer cannot be saved by the bell in any round, even the last
(d) the cut-off point for accidental fouls is four completed rounds
(e) there will be no scoring of an incomplete round, but point deductions which occur in that round will count.

The changes are fine as far as they go, but the lawyers will be kept busy by the rule which prevents a man being saved by the bell at the conclusion of the contracted twelve rounds. Once he has completed the distance for which he was hired and paid, he has surely fulfilled his contract in every respect, and court action will be bound to follow if a man is deprived of a world title – a significant commercial asset – in such dubious circumstances.

But at least it's a start, and after years of near-anarchy, when we have sometimes had to watch anxious fighters pace the ring for twenty minutes or more while officials from rival organisations pore over the small print of their respective rule books, any change for the better is welcome.

Dirty fighting is surprisingly rare in the ring, simply because it invites retaliation in kind and offers no guarantee that your retaliation will necessarily be any more effective than your opponent's. Most boxers will indulge in 'technical' fouls – trapping a man's glove, or leaning on excessively in clinches – but there have not been many who built their entire style around abuse of the rules.

Fritzie Zivic, welterweight champion from 1940–41, was the most famous exponent of the game's Black Arts, yet did it so cleverly that he was never disqualified in 232 fights and 18 years. (He claimed even more impressive statistics: 399 fights in 20 years.) Zivic was expert at what is known as 'working the referee's blind side' – committing fouls when the referee's view of the action is obscured, so that it becomes a simple choice of whom the official will believe: you or your opponent.

Sometimes the fouls have the tacit blessing of the referee, as Zivic recounted of his title-winning battle against Henry Armstrong. 'He was giving me the head and everything else, and the referee [Arthur Donovan] never warned him. After about five rounds I got mad and started to hit him low, choke him, foul him and everything else. Donovan stopped the fight in the sixth round, looked at Armstrong, looked at me and said "If you guys want to fight like this, it's OK with me."'

Zivic went on to give a master class in fouling, as he recalled to author Pete Heller in *In This Corner*. 'He'd have his head down trying to butt, so I'd come up on the side. When the eye was cut, I'd rub it with the laces to open it a little more. Then he's watching this cut and I'd cut his other eye.'

Yet even Zivic had his code of honour. 'I'd give 'em the head, choke 'em, hit 'em in the balls, but never in my life used the thumb because I wanted no one to use it on me. I used to bang 'em pretty good. You're fighting, you're not playing the piano, you know.'

Harry Gibbs, Britain's most famous post-war referee, was another who knew when to turn a judicious blind eye. Recalling a night in the early 1960s, he told me 'Don Johnson had just been given a very controversial decision over [British featherweight star] Howard Winstone at Olympia, and the crowd's mood was really ugly. It wouldn't have taken much to set them off.

'The next pair in were heavyweights Brian London, the former British champion, and Tom McNeeley of America. Halfway through the first round McNeeley gave him an awful butt, and put me in a quandary. If I'd disqualified him, as he deserved, the crowd would have gone potty. "Ref, he's butting me", London complained. "Well f...ing butt him back", I told him, and for the next two rounds they went at it like billygoats. At the start of the third I called them together and said "Right, lads, you've had your fun – now let's see some boxing", and for the rest of the way they behaved like perfect gentlemen.'

Sometimes a boxer's brutal speciality is all too apparent from his nickname, as in the case of turn-of-the-century lightweight George 'Elbows' McFadden. It was a fiercely competitive division then, and Joe Gans, Frank Erne and Kid Lavigne, three of the finest lightweight champions of their era, were all active. McFadden beat all three, but none of them happened to be holding the championship at that particular moment.

George's particular trick was to launch a roundhouse punch towards the jaw. It would miss, of course, but the following elbow would smash into the victim's mouth and leave him an easy mark for the legitimate knockout punch which completed the unorthodox combination. Like all the best fouls, the elbow would be delivered so fast that it was almost impossible to detect with the naked eye, and over the years McFadden refined the move to perfection.

One of the most notorious foul punches was the so-called pivot blow, a back-handed swing delivered as the boxer pivots on his heel. It was perfected by middleweight George LaBlanche, who used it to knock out Nonpareil Jack Dempsey in a title fight in August 1890. However, the manoeuvre was so blatantly illegal that the result was discounted and the blow banned. Anyone attempting to use it today would invite immediate disqualification.

Perhaps the dirtiest of all title fights was the fourth meeting between featherweight arch-rivals Willie Pep and Sandy Saddler, who was 2–1 ahead in their series going into their final encounter at the Polo Grounds, New York on 26 September 1951. Saddler, an abnormally tall featherweight, had acquired a reputation as a dirty fighter, specialising in opening cuts on opponents' eyes. He was not averse to 'heeling' with the glove – drawing the laced inside of the glove across his opponent's face, with almost inevitable damage.

Pep was supposedly a boxing genius, but he too could fight as rough as he had to and, on this occasion, both fighters conducted themselves as if they had made a pact to forget the rules entirely.

Pep developed a trick of trapping his man's feet and spinning him off-balance so that he would fall heavily, and he used the move extensively. Saddler was twice wrestled to the floor, at the end of the fifth and again in the eighth. Both fell over in the sixth, and referee Ray Miller was brought down as he tried to break up a seventh-round clinch, a round which Pep lost for 'unnecessary roughness'.

The *New York Times* commented: 'Any resemblance to the accepted theory of boxing as a "fair, stand-up exhibition" of skill between two perfectly-trained, well-matched, sportsmanlike individuals was surely coincidental in this brawl ... By some oversight, they failed to bite each other or to introduce that quaint kicking game – *la savate* – at one time very popular in France.'

Saddler admitted he'd fought dirty, but said 'I figured to fight cleanly and started to do so, but Pep started it. He was heeling, thumbing, stepping on my toes and wrestling all night.' At the end of the ninth Pep told referee Ray Miller he was unable to go on because his right eye, badly bruised and bloody, had troubled him from the second round.

A week later, the New York Commission revoked Pep's licence and suspended Saddler's indefinitely. Chairman Robert K. Christenberry told them 'You violated every rule in the book.' Pep told the hearing 'It seemed there was no referee in this fight. He was getting in too late to break us up. The only way I could get away from Saddler was to wrestle him. He was holding me by the head and banging away at my eyes.'

Sometimes a fighter acquires a brawler's reputation by accident rather than intent. Gene Fullmer, a rugged middleweight who was twice world champion between 1957–62, was a crude performer whose technical shortcomings meant that his battle plan had always to be simply to bang away at whatever target presented itself. Thus, he justified repeatedly rabbit-punching Sugar Ray Robinson by saying 'I'd sooner have hit him in the face than in the back of the head if he'd let go. It was his choice to get hit there. I didn't care where I hit him, and if he wanted to hold on so the only place I could hit him was the back of the head, I really didn't mind.'

Fullmer's round hard head served as an extra weapon, notably in foul-filled clashes with Joey Giardello and Carmen Basilio. He even suffered a fractured skull in his bruising draw against Giardello, the result of one such collision. 'Giardello admitted he butted me on purpose, because he wanted to win', he recalled. 'I never had one fighter say that I fought dirty. I mean, I fought crude and maybe it looked dirty to the spectators, but I never fought dirty.'

Australian heavyweight Peter Blackwell could offer no such defence. He began his pro career in style with a first-round knockout, yet never won another fight. He was stopped in his second, and his third, an Australian title fight, was so rough that referee Max Murphy declared it 'no contest' and the champion, Shane Raduly, announced that 'I'll never fight again while that animal is around.' The 'animal' went to New Zealand for his next two, being disqualified each time, and was rewarded with another shot at the vacant Australian title.

Far behind on points going into the final round, Blackwell seized opponent Tony Vickers in a headlock, wrestled him to the canvas, and resisted the efforts of three policemen and four seconds to disentangle them. Afterwards he apologised to referee Ray Mitchell, explaining that 'I'd rather be disqualified than knocked out.'

Many fighters have acted similarly – Mike Tyson in a rather more high-profile rematch with Evander Holyfield comes to mind – but few go to such extreme lengths to get out of a losing fight.

Amongst modern champions, Panamanian featherweight Eusebio Pedroza became known as a man with all the tricks. He won the WBA title in April 1978, and over the next eight years he defended it anywhere and everywhere, routinely conceding home advantage to eager young challengers. Perhaps he reasoned that such concessions entitled him to exercise a little leeway with the rules, for he acquired a fearsome reputation over the course of a record-breaking nineteen successful defences.

There is a sense of *déjà vu* about reading accounts of Pedroza's matches. Against Jose Caba, whom he outpointed in 1983, the champion was guilty of using his shoulders and elbows, hitting low, kidney punching and pulling his man's head onto right-handers. Against Juan LaPorte a year earlier, the charge sheet included low blows, kidney punching and elbowing, and so it went on. Yet Pedroza was also expert in a vital, and entirely legal, trick of the trade: he had the old pro's knack of doing just enough to sway the judges in a close round, and could time his late-round rally to the second.

When Pedroza signed to make his final defence against Ireland's Barry McGuigan, no angel himself, there were fears of an X-certificate brawl. McGuigan was a rib-bending body puncher, and if some of those strayed low – especially in the early stages, when no referee dare disqualify him – that was too bad. In fact, the pair battled like Corinthians, with never a foul on sight in fifteen utterly absorbing rounds. So much for reputation, and expectations.

One man who always delivered what he promised was Rocky Marciano, the roughest of all the heavyweight champions. Marciano compensated for his physical shortcomings with a merciless, hit-them-anywhere approach. He worked on the principle that even if his punches were only striking his opponent's forearms, they would eventually take their toll. Blood vessels in the arms would be ruptured, the hands would come down, exposing

Barry McGuigan's finest hour as the Irishman takes the WBA featherweight title from Panama veteran Eusebio Pedroza in 1985 the chin, and that would usually be that. He was a likeable man away from the ring, but utterly ruthless in it, and for sheer cynical disregard for the basic rules of behaviour in the ring, his title defence against English challenger Don Cockell – his penultimate fight – has never been surpassed.

He hit Cockell in the kidneys in the first round, punched after the bell to end the third, gashed his opponent's forehead with a butt in the fourth, hit him low in the fifth and sixth, punched him three times after the bell to end the sixth, butted and hit him low in the seventh, and rounded off his night's work by hitting him while he was down in the eighth.

'He never read the rule books', TV commentator Eamonn Andrews summarised. 'He played a different sport from the one Cockell had been taught ... a British referee would have sent him to his corner after three rounds.' Win, at all costs: no champion ever embodied that philosophy more vividly than the Rock, the only heavyweight champion to quit with a perfect record. His attitude may have been reprehensible, but it got results.

It is hard to imagine a more basic form of physical activity than boxing: after all, it consists of using your fists to punch your opponent and your reflexes to avoid being hit by him. Yet within that broad parameter there is so much rich and surprising scope for variation. Far from being basic, boxing is incredibly subtle and sophisticated, with as many ways to render the same movement as there are arrangements of classic songs. Just as the same piece of music will be handled entirely differently by Frank Sinatra, Willie Nelson, B.B. King or Bob Dylan, so boxing offers a complex variety of interpretations.

What, for example, does a punching machine like Jack Dempsey have in common with a delicate defensive artist like Herol Graham, a man capable of reducing strong and determined opponents to tears of frustrated rage? How does the classical

Herol Graham demonstrates his southpaw artistry

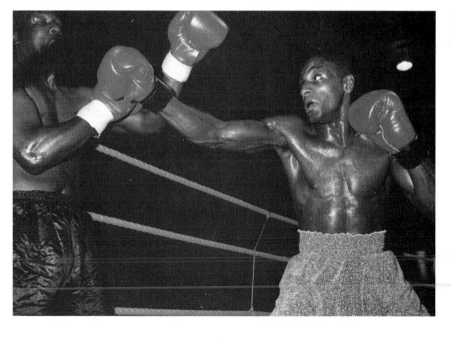

brilliance of Willie Pep, a man who once for a bet won a round without throwing a single punch, belong to the same sport as the clubbing Neanderthal aggression of Rocky Marciano? And then there are the players of 'mind games', a science first developed by Jack Johnson and refined by Muhammad Ali before, in its current high-profile embodiment, being taken over by Naseem Hamed.

They are all practising the same sport, improbable as it may seem at first glance, and the more one studies the subject the stronger becomes the attraction. Boxing has something for everyone, for all tastes, and if the style you're watching at the moment does not appeal, there will be another along in a minute.

Perhaps we tend to favour the styles which most reflect our own personality, real or fantasised: certainly boxing judges who were once fighters themselves will almost invariably lean towards the man whose style mirrors their own. Crafty counter-punchers are unlikely to give the nod to face-first sluggers, nor will sharp left-jabbers like Larry Holmes be overly impressed by the one-hit wonders of someone like George Foreman or Earnie Shavers.

The style a boxer will use throughout his career is usually moulded from his first days in the amateur gym, when a good coach will study what a boy does instinctively well and build on his strengths rather than concentrate on his weaknesses. It is normally easy to tell whether a boy is a natural puncher, although that rule is not inflexible. It took a coach of Emanuel Steward's genius to realise that behind the light-punching, flitting style of the amateur Thomas Hearns was one of the great hitters of the modern era. Steward insists, contrary to popular belief, that great punchers can be manufactured, and how can you argue with such spectacular results?

During the long years of the Cold War, the Eastern bloc countries tended to dominate amateur competitions with their rigidly orthodox, stiff-backed style. Right cross would follow left jab like an automaton, and any attempt to develop individual flair or variety was frowned upon. Curiously, though, the system collapsed when the Eastern bloc coaches working in Cuba tried to impose their brand of dour discipline on a hugely-talented group of laid-back Caribbean athletes. They had to acknowledge defeat and allow the Cubans to express themselves in the ring in the

Thomas Hearns (right) against Sugar Ray Leonard is one of the great punchers of his era yet rarely scored a knockout as an amateur colourful and extrovert way which came most naturally to them. The result was a glut of Olympic and world championships.

The Cubans even started to export their own coaches, with instant results. It was no coincidence that Ireland won her first boxing gold medal through welterweight Michael Carruth after a Cuban, Nicholas Hernandez Cruz, had been placed in charge of the country's preparations in 1989 ... or that Cuba won seven golds at those same 1992 Games. (By a delicious irony, Carruth beat a Cuban, Juan Hernandez, in the final.)

Now that the Eastern bloc system has gone, we may see a flowering of the natural individualistic talent which has surely been there all along. In Cuba, too, we may expect a resurgence of professional boxing once the Castro era ends. The late 1950s were golden years for Cuban boxing with stars like Kid Gavilan, Jose Napoles, Sugar Ramos, Florentino Fernandez and Doug Vailliant all either world champions or contenders. Most had to emigrate to Mexico or America to continue their careers once the barriers went up, but the explosion of capitalism which will almost certainly mark Castro's departure will also signal the country's return as a major force in world professional boxing.

Fighters' styles evolve in different ways. Sometimes it reflects the personal preferences of the trainer, with youngsters being taught almost by numbers. Such methods rarely produce champions, but an intelligently-practised variation on them can. Back in the 1970s an experienced ringside observer would be able to identify a boxer schooled by Terry Lawless, who ran the country's most successful stable, just by the way he held himself in the ring. Similarly today, a protégé of Brendan Ingle's wildly unconventional boxing academy in Sheffield is equally unmistakable.

Ingle does not teach his boys to be clones of each other, but he lays down a template within which they develop. He places emphasis on unpredictability, on being equally at home in a conventional or southpaw stance. His boxers will attempt punches from impossible angles, and because they are impossible they will connect. He demands discipline and loyalty, which are important considerations given the type of deprived background from which so many of his boxers come.

To an extent, their ring style is moulded by how desperate they are to escape their environment, just as boxing has always offered an honest route to a better life. Kid Gavilan and Kid Chocolate (the featherweight star of the 1930s), the two finest products of Cuban boxing, both claimed to have developed their trademark 'bolo' punch in the same way. By the age of ten, Cuban youngsters like them were working in the sugar cane fields, swinging the seven-pound bolo knife which, Gavilan always claimed, was how he devised the 'bolo' punch – a half-hook, half-uppercut delivered with a whipping action. True or not – and there is no reason to doubt him – it made great copy for American boxing writers of the day.

Boxing has always been a poor man's sport. It requires no complicated and expensive training aids, no electronic timing devices, no huge entourage (although this will inevitably form around the successful young star). What boxing demands, primarily, is the hunger to make the grade and the courage to endure setbacks and disappointments. Self-belief is a prerequisite: if a man does not believe absolutely in his own ability, how can he persuade others to do so for him?

For the rare genius, like Muhammad Ali (Cassius Clay, as he then was), self-belief carried to an absurd degree was central to his development and his style. He believed, without even a nagging doubt, that he could not be beaten or even hurt, a conviction which did not waver in the face of the best left hook Henry Cooper ever threw. It takes a terrifying level of

Even Muhammad Ali's defensive skill could not prevent Henry Cooper's jab from landing on target.

concentration to live on the edge in the way that he did in the ring, knowing that one split-second lapse, one infinitesimal miscalculation of range or distance, would bring instant calamity.

He got away with it through the early years, until his opposition to the Vietnam War drove him out of boxing. When he returned three years later, the erosion had begun. He was still phenomenally quick, but now the margins by which he made his opponents' punches miss were shrinking, ominously. Eventually, of course, the bill had to be paid, as the dreadful blows he took from a murderous generation like Foreman, Shavers, Norton, Quarry and the rest destroyed the finest athlete ever to grace the ring.

His acolytes, like Chris Eubank and Naseem Hamed, have tried to erect the same kind of shield of self-belief around themselves, with varying degrees of success. Eubank set out to project himself as the Man You Love To Hate, and found there was indeed a niche in the market for an old-style wresting villain. His ever more outrageous antics were designed to unsettle and irritate his opponent as much as the crowd, and it succeeded at all levels. He worked hard at his 'mind games', and seemed to feed off the hostility he generated as, for example, when he prowled the ring during an interval rather than sit in his corner.

It helped, of course, that he could really fight when he had to, and no one who witnessed his epic struggles with Nigel Benn and Michael Watson dare question the purity of his fighting soul. His relationship with his public grew ever more complex as they gradually came to recognise his real worth: they came to jeer, and stayed to cheer.

The increase in his popularity coincided with the gradual decline in his abilities. Steve Collins, a no-nonsense Irishman, outpsyched him and took his WBO super-middleweight title in Cork, and things would never be the same again. (What on earth possessed Eubank to think he could beat an Irishman in Cork on St Patrick's weekend? Self-belief of that intensity defies logic, not to mention historical precedent: the only other Irishman to win a world title in his home country, light-heavyweight Mike McTigue, did so on 17 March 1923.)

Eternal optimist...Chris Eubank thought he could beat Irish challenger Steve Collins (right) on St Patrick's weekend. He was wrong

Naseem Hamed is still young enough and fresh enough to get away with his own particular brand of living on the edge, although his shaky victory over Kevin Kelley in December 1997 offered a dramatic reminder that even he cannot afford to neglect the basics of self-defence. Hamed illustrates the theory that a man's ring style can be determined by his physical characteristics. In his case, his greatest asset are his legs, over which boxing people drool the way their grandfathers did over Betty Grable's famous pins half a century ago. Legs are vital to a boxer. Everything flows from there: strength, balance, stamina and power, and Hamed has perfect legs, which belong on a middleweight.

For other fighters, their physical shape and dimensions predetermine their ring style. Short heavyweights like Rocky Marciano, Joe Frazier or Mike Tyson were, of necessity, aggressive sluggers who had to get inside their opponent's longer reach and, resting their head on their man's shoulder, rip in short-range hooks. Conversely, a 6ft 6ins heavyweight like Ernie Terrell, WBA champion in the mid-1960s, could never hope to be a brawler. He had to make the best use he could of his assets, such as they were, and utilised his height and reach to make himself the most awkward heavyweight of his era.

Others, like two-time heavyweight champion Floyd Patterson, will choose to ignore a flaw in their own fighting make-up if it suits them to do so. Patterson, throughout his twenty-year career, suffered from bad balance in the ring, which resulted in him suffering more knockdowns than any other heavyweight king. Yet he knew that if he worked on his balance, slowing himself down to settle for his punches, he would forfeit his greatest asset, which was his extraordinary hand speed. Sometimes Patterson would actually launch a combination while in mid-air, having leapt at his opponent with both feet off the ground. The move would never be found in any text-book, but it suited Patterson's quirky nature and style and his mentor, the equally strange and intense Cus D'Amato, was happy to let him continue so long as it worked.

Most intelligent trainers will share D'Amato's attitude, and recognise that, ultimately, a boxer's style will evolve from within the man himself. A trainer can nurture and encourage, but a fighter's style must always be his own, as individual as his fingerprints.

Floyd Patterson, taking a count against Muhammad Ali, was floored more often than any other heavyweight champion

All sports have their landmark events, the milestones which trace the game's development. Boxing is such a dramatic and endlessly absorbing spectacle that a host of great fights clamour for inclusion in our top ten, but the quality of the fight is not the sole criterion. Marvin Hagler v Thomas Hearns, arguably the most thrilling championship clash in boxing history, did not make the final cut, while infinitely duller spectacles like **Jack Johnson**'s defeat of **Tommy Burns** in 1908 did. That one-sided affair merits its place because it smashed the odious colour bar which had operated in the heavyweight division since gloved boxing began, and because it marked the start of the reign of the sport's most controversial standard-bearer.

Another mismatch, **Jack Dempsey** v **Georges Carpentier**, is there because it was the first million-dollar gate, and in professional boxing nothing matters more than the money. **Henry Armstrong**'s 1938 win over **Lou Ambers** left him holding three world titles simultaneously, a feat which the rules of the sport today prohibit. This was the first time it had been achieved, and the last.

Joe Louis' revenge win over **Max Schmeling** in 1938 assumed a significance far beyond the ring, as the fighters were projected as representatives of rival ideologies. Sport has too often been used as a metaphor for war, but never as nakedly as on this famous occasion.

The passing of a great champion is as much a landmark as the coronation of another, and **Rocky Marciano**'s final fight and **Cassius Clay**'s title win, in 1955 and 1964 respectively, are noteworthy for that reason. Sandwiched between them is **Floyd**

Patterson's 1960 defeat of **Ingo Johansson** to become the first man to regain the heavyweight championship. Patterson was already the youngest heavyweight king, and this made him twice a history-maker.

The start of the **Ray Leonard** v **Roberto Duran** rivalry, in 1980, was significant for two reasons: one, that Duran's performance in victory marked him as one of the finest fighters of all time, and two, that Leonard's showing in defeat moulded him into the unforgettable performer he became.

Mike Tyson seemed destined for greatness on a scale above even Duran and Leonard's, until **Buster Douglas** shattered the myth of Iron Mike in 1990. It was boxing's biggest upset, and a vivid reminder of how quickly fortunes and reputations are made and destroyed in this unforgiving business. Tennis players can lose half a dozen major tournament finals and still be ranked with the best, but in boxing it only takes one defeat to undermine a lifetime's work.

Our final entry, **Naseem Hamed**'s 1997 knockout of **Kevin Kelley** in their Madison Square Garden thriller, is included because of the winner's potential to become the greatest English fighter of his generation. If he succeeds in earning that recognition, his dramatic American debut will be acknowledged as the cornerstone of his career.

1908: JACK JOHNSON BREAKS THE COLOUR BAR

Few champions had it tougher than Jack Johnson. It took him years to be given the title shot his talent merited, and as champion he became the most reviled figure in boxing history. His every victory sparked off race riots and lynchings across America, and prejudice drove him into exile. If his own account is to be believed, he was eventually tricked out of his title by agreeing to take a dive in return for avoiding a jail sentence in a case for which he should never have been prosecuted in the first place.

Yet history has been kinder to him, and today he stands alongside Joe Louis and Muhammad Ali in the pantheon of black ring heroes. For Ali, in particular, Johnson was a role model in social attitude as well as boxing technique, and he remains a pivotal figure in the sport's development. He was the man who smashed the colour barrier so shamefully erected by John L. Sullivan, whose ignoble boast that 'I never fought a nigger and I never will' drew the line behind which all his successors as champion stood.

Johnson, a former dock labourer from Galveston, had been born a mere fifteen years after slavery had been abolished, yet he refused to play by the white man's rules and consequently made his path to the top even harder than it need have been. In an era when fight reports routinely used terms like 'coon', 'blackie' and 'Sambo' when referring to black fighters, it was doubly difficult for someone like Johnson, who actively courted unpopularity by his preference for white women, to attract backing and sympathy from the exclusively white-owned press. But he persevered, compiling such an impressive record that even his many enemies were finally forced to acknowledge his right to a title chance. But champion Tommy Burns, a squat Canadian who had won the title in 1906 and made eleven successful defences, was in no rush to accommodate him. He knew that the longer he delayed the match, the more lucrative it would become and he allowed Johnson to pursue him across the world from America to England and, finally, Australia before accepting his challenge and facing him at Rushcutter's Bay, Sydney on 26 December 1908.

He extracted a then-huge purse of $30,000 from promoter High D. McIntosh, whose initials earned him the nickname 'Huge Deal', and Johnson made him earn every cent of it as he gave the outclassed champion a fearful, one-sided beating. Johnson toyed with him, taunted him, talked to him and declined a dozen chances to put him out of his misery until finally the local police inspector entered the ring in the fourteenth round, fearing an imminent riot, and ordered the fight to be stopped. Johnson had smashed the colour bar – but his turbulent reign caused its re-erection, and the world would have to wait until Joe Louis in 1937 for its second black heavyweight champion.

1921: JACK DEMPSEY DRAWS THE FIRST MILLION-DOLLAR GATE

Jack Dempsey is remembered as one of boxing's best-loved and most charismatic champions, so it is ironic that in the fight in which he drew the first million-dollar gate he was seen very much as the bad guy. Georges Carpentier, the glamorous and handsome Frenchman who faced him on that historic afternoon at Boyle's Thirty Acres, New Jersey, was a distinguished war hero who had won the *Croix de Guerre*, while Dempsey had been labelled as a draft dodger after a publicity photo, designed to show him helping the war effort by working in a shipyard, revealed that he was wearing

GEORGES CARPENTIER

His cameo-like profile, tall, beautifully proportioned figure; made him an attractive personality, with the suppleness of a panther. His combat with Jack Dempsey, the lion-like fighter, will never be erased from boxing history. It was not generally known that Carpentier broke his thumb in this encounter. Over anxiety to which great boxers are prone, was his weakness.

patent leather shoes at the time. The subsequent furore saw Dempsey indicted by a Federal Grand Jury for draft evasion, and, even though he was acquitted, the public mood was firmly against him.

Promoter Tex Rickard, who had the stadium specially built for the event, manipulated the press brilliantly, selling the match as a clash of opposites: the sophisticated, debonair Frenchman against the scowling ex-hobo; combat veteran against shirker; the Old World against the New. The publicity succeeded beyond anyone's expectations, and the 80,000 crowd who crammed into the makeshift arena on 2 July paid a staggering $1,789,238, of which Dempsey was guaranteed $300,000.

A record 700 journalists from around the world covered the fight, which was also the first title fight to be broadcast. Neither man was a heavyweight by today's standards: Dempsey, in his third defence of the title he had taken from Jess Willard in July 1919, scaled two pounds inside the modern cruiserweight limit at 13 st 6 lbs, while Carpentier, who held the world light-heavyweight title, was two pounds inside that division's limit at 12 st 4 lbs.

Dempsey opened at his usual frantic pace, bullying the slender challenger around the ring and hammering to his ribs, but Carpentier – a fierce hitter in his own weight class – landed a stunning right in the second which almost floored the champion. Dempsey was desperately hurt, but he held on and mauled his way through the rest of the round. The Frenchman's chance had come and gone, for that mighty right had smashed his thumb on Dempsey's head, and there was no way he could survive one-handed against an opponent as relentless as the Manassa Mauler.

JACK DEMPSEY
Former Champion of the World. A truly wonderful boxer at his best, cheery, smiling, unwisely confident, and a man of supreme physical fitness. A lover of books, and an enthusiastic conversationalist on literature. This big, clever fellow conquered Georges Carpentier in four rounds before 90,000 spectators, in that memorable encounter, when the lion defeated the panther.

The third was brutally one-sided, with only Carpentier's courage keeping him on his feet, and his challenge faded a round later as Dempsey floored him for eight with a left hook and then finished the job with a right to the body. As soon as referee Harry Ertle had completed the final count, Dempsey uncharacteristically rushed to Carpentier's aid and helped him to his corner, a sporting gesture which did much to alleviate the crowd's hostility towards him.

1938: HENRY ARMSTRONG BECOMES A TRIPLE CHAMPION

Triple champions are commonplace in the modern era, when the multiplicity of so-called governing bodies means there are twelve versions of seventeen championships on offer. But when Henry Armstrong won his third title on 17 August 1938, there were just nine divisions, each with a single champion – and what made Armstrong's feat all the more remarkable is that he held his three titles simultaneously, across a weight spread of 21lbs, from featherweight to welterweight. And is if that unmatched achievement was not enough, he then fought a draw for a version of the middleweight championship!

HENRY ARMSTRONG
Born at St. Louis, Mo. Dec. 12th, 1912.
American, won the Featherweight Championship of the World, Oct. 27th, 1936. In 1937 he successfully defended this title against Pete Sarron. On May 31st, 1938 he outpointed Barney Ross and won a second World's title — the Welter-weight Championship. Beat Lou Ambers for Light-weight Title, Aug. 1938. Is first Boxer to hold three world titles at the same time.

There was nothing in Armstrong's early career to indicate future greatness. Born Henry Jackson, the youngest of eleven children, he moved to St Louis with his family when the Mississippi cotton crop failed. After a brief amateur career he turned pro as Mellody Jackson, taking the name of the old welterweight champion Honey Mellody, but fared dismally with three defeats in four fights. He rode the rails west to Los Angeles, re-entered the amateurs as Henry Armstrong, and acquired a reputation for a prodigious work-rate which saw him go undefeated in eighty-five contests in 1931, winning sixty-six of them inside the distance.

When he relaunched his pro career, his progress was meteoric and, in October 1937, he knocked out Petey Sarron to become featherweight champion, a title he never defended. He struggled to make 9st, but instead of moving up to lightweight he skipped straight to welterweight and took that title from one of the division's legendary champions, Barney Ross. Three months later, he stepped down a division to challenge Lou Ambers in Madison Square Garden, New York for the lightweight crown in front of a standing-room-only crowd of 20,000.

Armstrong had suffered a bad cut on his lower lip in sparring with an old opponent Chalky Wright, the former featherweight champion, and the wound reopened in the third of the scheduled fifteen rounds against Ambers. To keep the blood from showing, and thus giving Ambers encouragement and perhaps even forcing the referee to stop the fight, Armstrong kept swallowing the blood for the remaining twelve rounds, which weakened him considerably.

Ambers was floored twice, in the fifth and sixth rounds, but bounced up to keep the pressure on the challenger. Armstrong's left eye was cut in the thirteenth, and his nose was also bleeding heavily, but he sensed the champion had shot his bolt and mounted a sustained assault over the final two rounds, which earned him the narrowest of wins. The judges were split, 7–6–2 and 8–7 for Armstrong, 8–7 for Ambers, but Henry had his third title and his place with the immortals.

1938: JOE LOUIS TAKES REVENGE

When Max Schmeling knocked out Joe Louis in twelve rounds in June 1936, he did much more than merely win a fight: he shattered the hopes of American blacks, for whom the undefeated young Detroit puncher had become an icon. Louis had won twenty-seven in a row, twenty-four by knockout including victories over two former world champions in Primo Carnera and Max Baer. His progress had been so spectacular that there seemed a real chance that, after the long years of discrimination since Jack Johnson's reign ended in 1915, a black fighter might once again be given the chance to become champion.

But Schmeling, a wily old pro who had been champion from 1930–32, detected a defensive weakness in the youngster: when he threw a left jab he tended to be slow in pulling the left back to guard the chin, and the German took full advantage to land right after right over Louis' lead. Joe was floored in the fourth – his first knockdown as a pro – and badly rocked in the fifth and sixth. He rallied in the middle rounds, but took a fearful beating in the eleventh and twelfth before Schmeling knocked him out in two minutes 29 seconds of the round. 'He must have hit me with about fifty right hands that round', Louis recalled ruefully.

Louis roared back with seven straight victories which carried him to the title: he knocked out James J. Braddock to become champion a year and three days after losing to Schmeling. But even though he retained the title with three quick defences, Louis insisted 'I won't be the champion until I've beaten Schmeling', and the rematch was set for 22 June 1938 at Yankee Stadium, New York.

JOE LOUIS
Born May 13th, 1914 at Lexington, Ala. He won the heavy-weight Champion- ship of the World, June 22nd, 1937, by defeating James J. Braddock, on a K.O. in 8 rounds at Chicago. Louis has successfully defended his title against Tommy Farr and Max Schmeling and looks likely to remain Champion for some years to come as there does not seem any other boxer in his class.

By then, political considerations had overtaken the significance of the event as just a championship fight. Schmeling was depicted by Dr Goebbels' Nazi propaganda machine as a symbol of Hitler's Master Race, while the powerful Jewish lobby in America helped project the fight as some kind of holy war between rival ideologies.

The rematch drew 70,000 fans, paying a total of $1,015,012, and they saw Louis deliver the defining, perfect performance of his majestic career. In 124 destructive seconds, Schmeling was floored three times. The radio link to Germany was pulled off the air as the challenger's shrieks of agony were clearly audible when a right which landed on his back smashed two vertebrae. Louis' revenge was complete, and now he *could* call himself the champion ... for the next ten years.

1955: THE ROCK CHECKS OUT

After forty-eight straight wins, and without an obvious challenger on the horizon, Rocky Marciano was losing interest. Constant money squabbles with his manager, Al Weill, and the domestic strain of spending long months away from home in training camp, sapped his enthusiasm for the game even further. The only man who might have given him a worthwhile test, the giant Cuban Nino Valdes, was outsmarted in a 15-round eliminator by veteran light-heavyweight champion Archie Moore, who kept manoeuvring Valdes around the open-air ring in Las Vegas so that the sun was constantly in the Cuban's eyes.

Moore had long harboured heavyweight ambitions, and the win over Valdes gave his challenge some credibility. More importantly, Archie was a

MAX SCHMELING.
Born Luckow, Germany, Sept. 28th, 1905. He won heavy-weight Championship of the World, June 12, 1930 from Jack Sharkey. On June 21st, 1932, he met Sharkey again for the title and lost on points. In 1936 he knocked out Joe Louis before Louis was world's Champion, in 12 rounds. Louis gained his revenge, as he knocked out Schmeling inside one round, at New York on June 22, 1938, in defence of his title.

81

Rocky Marciano ignored the rule book, and quit with a perfect record

brilliant self-publicist, who launched a determined campaign to persuade the public that, despite his 41 years and 190 recorded fights, he had a genuine chance to become the first light-heavyweight to win the heavyweight championship. (Bob Fitzsimmons had completed the double in reverse, becoming light-heavyweight king after losing the senior title.)

Like Marciano, Moore had run out of challengers in his own division and his knockout record – 120 in 190 fights – was so impressive that the match, at New York's Yankee Stadium on 21 September 1955, captured the imagination. Only the Battle of the Long Count between Gene Tunney and Jack Dempsey, thirty years previously, drew higher receipts, as 61,574 fans paid $2,248,117 to watch a clash which lived up to all expectations.

The thrills came thick and fast. In the second round, Moore stepped inside a Marciano left and dropped the champion with a classic, short right-hand counter. The standing eight count, normally operative in New York, had been waived for this fight, but referee Harry Kessler apparently forgot, and gave the dazed Marciano the full benefit of the eight seconds after he had risen, unsteadily, at two. Moore was one of the game's greatest finishers, and would have had every chance of scoring a huge upset, but Marciano recovered quickly and, from the third, began to break up the challenger with a steamroller attack, pounding blows onto whatever target area presented itself.

Moore was floored twice in the sixth and again at the end of the eighth, and between rounds the Commission doctor invited him to accept the inevitable and surrender. 'I too am a champion', he replied memorably, 'and I'll go down fighting.' A minute later, it was over as a final stream of hooks put the veteran down for the final time. Archie fought on until 1963, and challenged again for the heavyweight title against Floyd Patterson in 1956, but the Rock had had enough and, on 21 April 1956, Marciano bowed out with what remains the only perfect record in heavyweight history: forty-nine fights, forty-nine wins, forty-three inside the distance.

1960: PATTERSON BREAKS THE JINX

The betting odds, and the cold statistics in the record books, said Floyd Patterson had no chance of regaining the world heavyweight title from the handsome Swede Ingemar (Ingo) Johansson, who had humiliated him with a seven-knockdown, three rounds stoppage in New York in June 1959. A long and depressing list of Patterson's predecessors had tried and failed to regain the championship, stretching all the way back to James J. Corbett in 1900 and including Bob Fitzsimmons, James J. Jeffries, Jack Dempsey, Max Schmeling, Joe Louis, Ezzard Charles and Jersey Joe Walcott. There was a jinx at work, and the fragile-chinned Patterson, who took a total of seventeen counts during his championship career, and had even been floored by professional debutant Pete Rademacher, seemed particularly ill-equipped to smash it.

Johansson, the first European to win the title since Primo Carnera in 1933, was unbeaten in twenty-one fights and possessed a thunderous right which he called 'Ingo's Bingo'. He was a wildly unorthodox professional, who outraged accepted wisdom by having his beautiful girl-friend Birgit live with him in training camp. As champion, the fun-loving Swede took a year off to enjoy his glory, while the loser, a complex and obsessive man, retreated into seclusion to brood on his defeat and prepare for the rematch, at the Polo Grounds in New York – his home town – on 20 June 1960.

He lived like a hermit for twelve months, locked away with his mentor Cus D'Amato (who discovered Mike Tyson twenty years later) as they endlessly reviewed the mistakes which had cost him the title and worked on their eradication. The result was the finest performance of Patterson's twenty-year career. He fought with an intensity of focus and a controlled fury, dazzling the champion with his hand speed and keeping him off-balance with jabs, denying him leverage to fire that destructive right.

In the fifth round, two crushing left hooks sent Johansson sprawling on his back, blood trickling from the corner of his mouth and his leg twitching in uncontrollable spasms. Patterson thrust his arms aloft in triumph as the champion was counted out after one minute fifty-one seconds of the round, and then realised to his horror how badly hurt the Swede was. Happily, Johansson quickly regained his senses, but the moment had frightened the sensitive Patterson so much that he never again fought with the ferocity he showed on the night he rewrote the history books.

1964: THE START OF THE ALI ERA

Unless you lived through the years when Charles 'Sonny' Liston dominated the heavyweight division, it is hard to evoke the menace the man conveyed, the aura of invincibility which surrounded him. Liston was the best in the world

Muhammad Ali

for at least three years before champion Floyd Patterson finally gave him a title shot in 1962, and Liston needed only 126 seconds to prove the point. Patterson lasted four seconds longer in the rematch in July 1963.

Sonny was a mystery man, from the toughest of backgrounds. He had twenty-four half-brothers and sisters, and was raised in dreadful poverty in Arkansas before moving with his mother to St Louis. His birth went unrecorded and his true age was always in debate, with many believing him much older than his acknowledged birth date of 8 May 1932.

He ran wild on the St Louis streets, and inevitably finished up in jail for armed robbery. Prison proved his salvation, as the Catholic chaplain there, Fr. Charles Stephens, took an interest in the illiterate, friendless teenager and encouraged him to take up boxing. He turned professional after being paroled in 1963, but never managed to leave his past behind him and was constantly harassed by the law.

Even so, he was improbably cast as the good guy when he signed to defend against the loudmouth upstart Cassius Clay, the Olympic light-heavyweight champion in 1960, whose poems, predictions and highly inventive ring style had alienated as many fans as they attracted. Clay had beaten everyone put before him, usually naming the round in which he would win, but the fact that he had been floored and almost knocked out by England's Henry Cooper in his final fight before facing Liston at Miami Beach on 25 February 1964 did not bode well for his chances against the powerful champion, whose left jab alone was a knockout weapon.

Sonny Liston

Clay caused uproar at the weigh-in, acting like a madman and persuading the Commission doctor that 'He's scared to death. He's emotionally unbalanced, liable to crack up before he enters the ring.' Ten minutes later Clay reappeared, completely calm and normal, and Liston was hopelessly confused. That night the once-formidable champion fought like a man in a daze, plodding aimlessly around the ring and being picked off by whipping jabs and hooks from the fleet-footed challenger. Clay's only fright came in the fifth round when ointment from Liston's cut eye somehow found its way onto the champion's gloves and into Clay's eyes, causing temporary blurring of his vision.

Clay's speed and variety of punches bewildered the big man until Liston (left) refused to come out for the seventh round

Trainer Angelo Dundee ordered him to 'run like a thief' until the eyes had cleared, and by the end of the sixth he had recovered so well that Liston, bleeding and demoralised, slumped on his stool at the bell and refused to come out for the seventh.

The title was Clay's, and next day he shocked the world again by renouncing his 'slave name'. He announced he would henceforth be known as Cassius X, and then, shortly afterwards, took the name which became the most famous in all of sports: Muhammad Ali.

1980: THE MAKING OF SUGAR RAY

Sometimes – rarely – winner and loser both leave the ring with their reputations enhanced. That was certainly the case when Roberto Duran, who had already proved himself the best lightweight of all time with a record-equalling twelve defences, stepped up to welterweight to dethrone the unbeaten Olympic Golden Boy, Ray Leonard, in Montreal.

Duran, whose Hands of Stone nickname was well earned, was a pure fighting animal, a rugged brawler who could box with the best when he had to, but who loved nothing more than getting down in the trenches and breaking his opponent's spirit. He was in his prime at twenty-nine, while Leonard – who won his 1976 Olympic gold medal in the same Montreal ring – was a youngster of twenty-four. Leonard was the TV darling, a handsome and articulate man who projected himself brilliantly. He was already a millionaire many times over, from his advertising work as well as his twenty-six consecutive victories, and he earned another £3.5m for the Duran defence. The challenger got £650,000, but the Panamanian had the powerful incentive of winning his second title.

Leonard was seen as what the American fans call 'a Fancy Dan', a stylist who perhaps lacked the strength to compete on Duran's terms, and the criticism gnawed at him. It suited Duran anyway to rile Leonard and disrupt his cool tactical plans, and he even insulted the champion's wife during the build-up. The ploy worked: in his anxiety to prove his worth as a fighting man, and to punish Duran for his taunts and sneers, Leonard neglected his boxing and went head-to-head with the toughest competitor in the business.

The result was a wildly exciting battle, fifteen rounds of relentless action as Duran charged into Leonard, fists pumping and coal-black hair flying. Leonard could have outboxed him, as he clearly proved in their two subsequent encounters, but this time he tried to do it the hard way and paid for it with his title, as Duran took a desperately close but unanimous decision with scores of 145–144, 148–147 and 146–144. At the final bell Leonard

Victory in defeat: Sugar Ray Leonard lost his welterweight title to Roberto Duran in this Montreal thriller but profited so much from the experience that he became a complete fighter in the process

offered his glove, but Duran shoved him aside contemptuously. There was no room for civility in his bleak world, only the joy of combat and the exultation of victory.

Leonard noted the snub, and stored it away with all the other bitter memories for which he would exact such complete revenge in the rematch three months later when a demoralised Duran would do the unthinkable and walk out of the fight in the eighth round, shouting '*No mas*' ('No more'). Leonard had lost the decision this time, but had become the finished, polished product in the process.

1990: THE TYSON MYTH CRUMBLES

Mike Tyson was unravelling, personally and professionally, at an alarming rate when he agreed to defend against the mediocre James 'Buster' Douglas on 11 February 1990. But what no one fully understood was the speed at which it was happening, and the Las Vegas odds-makers duly installed Douglas as a derisory 42–1 outsider. On the face of it, the odds were justified. Douglas, the son of 1960s pro Billy Douglas, had some ability but seemed to have settled for life as a 'name opponent' after blowing his only previous title chance. Fighting Tony Tucker for the vacant IBF belt, Douglas boxed well for a few rounds but then lost his way and quit abruptly in the tenth round.

Life had treated him harshly since then. Just twenty-three days before the Tyson fight his mother died of a stroke; his wife had left him, and the mother of his eleven-year-old son was dying of cancer. Such griefs and distractions could have swamped him, but instead he used the fight as a means of escaping them and immersed himself in training, to such effect that he entered the ring in superb condition for the first time in his career.

Tyson had his problems, too, but the crucial difference was that he brought them into the ring with him. His marriage had collapsed, and so too had his relationship with the original team who had steered him to the championship. Instead, he replaced experienced professionals like trainer Kevin Rooney with know-nothing amateurs, with the result that the man for whom training was once a matter of pride turned up in Japan looking soft and ill-prepared, and without a single seasoned pro to direct events in his corner and plan strategy.

One-hit wonder Buster Douglas (right) wrecks Mike Tyson's record with a tenth-round knockout

Douglas, alone amongst Tyson's opponents so far, fought without fear: after what he had endured, anything Tyson could do to him would be a mere distraction. He easily outboxed the plodding champion in the early rounds, and by the fourth, Tyson's left eye was starting to swell. By the time the fight ended, it would be shut almost to a slit.

Douglas staged the perfect tactical fight, snapping jabs into Tyson's face to keep him off-balance and whipping right uppercuts which were the ideal counter to Tyson's crouching attacks. Without anyone to suggest alternative tactics, the panic mounted in the champion's corner as even their uneducated eyes could see the title was slipping away.

Tyson took matters into his own hands in the eighth, dropping the challenger on his back with a classic right uppercut. Referee Octavio Meyran was slow to pick up the count and Douglas – as he was perfectly entitled to do – stayed down until Meyran reached 'nine', by which time he had actually been on the floor for thirteen seconds. He made a splendid recovery, going back to his steady breaking-up process until, in the tenth, Tyson could take no more. He fell to his knees from a four-punch combination, and was counted out as he struggled to pick up and replace his gumshield.

1997: HAMED TAKES NEW YORK BY STORM

The English are supposedly under-stated and discreet, while the Americans are brash and over-the-top, so there was a delicious irony in the fact that the most colourful and extravagant performer in modern boxing, Naseem Hamed from Sheffield, encountered so much hostility when he went to New York to make his American debut in December 1997. Maybe it was because the Americans will only tolerate his brand of showmanship when it is practised by one of their own, or because nobody had yet tried anything like the full-blown Hamed ring entrance. Whatever the reason, it looked at first as though Naz would be a hard sell for his promoter Frank Warren, who hired the sport's most famous venue, Madison Square Garden, for what was also his first American venture.

Garden officials estimated that the fight on 19 December would only draw around 6,000, even though the opponent, former WBC champion Kevin Kelley, was a local fighter with a fine record and an ego just marginally smaller than the WBO champion's. This was the first stage of a $12.5m deal HBO, the pay-per-view TV company, had concluded with Warren and they invested hugely in advertising the event. A massive cut-out of Hamed towered over Times Square, and there were endless TV commercials. Hamed played his part to the full with a string of outrageous quotes and headline-grabbing stunts, and in the week leading up to the fight one could sense a swing in the public's mood towards him. The press were almost unanimously favourable, and that was reflected in the ticket sales.

By fight time there were almost 13,000 in the Garden, a stunning achievement by all concerned, and they were about to see an event which, for once, surpassed anticipation. Kelley stood on the ropes gesturing to Hamed to hurry up, as the champion posed and danced in silhouette behind a giant screen before starting his ring walk through a blizzard of confetti.

The whole performance dripped with arrogance – which was why it must have seemed like his worst nightmare when Hamed suddenly found himself on his back from a Kelley right. He stumbled through the round, his defence in tatters, and there was no hint of improvement in the second, as Kelley dropped him again for another eight count. It was Hamed's supreme crisis, the moment which could make or wreck his career, and he responded magnificently with a lead right which dumped the American in a shocked heap.

Naseem Hamed (right) comes through the crisis to crush Kevin Kelley in Hamed's American debut

They took turns to rock each other in a blistering third round, before the climax came in the fourth. Hamed sent the challenger crashing on his side with a left, and Kelley decided attack was the best form of defence and promptly floored Hamed for the third time when a right made the off-balance Englishman's glove brush the canvas. Technically it counted as a knockdown, but Kelley was the one in trouble as Hamed drove him back in the last thirty seconds, a final left hook crumpling the New Yorker onto his back. He got to his knees and seemed capable of beating the count, but referee Benji Esteves signalled 'out' an instant before Kelley was upright.

It hadn't been pretty, or technical, and Hamed's defensive deficiencies were worryingly exposed, but those privileged to be there knew they had witnessed one of the great brawls in featherweight history. Hamed had conquered his New World.

A specific language has grown up around boxing since the days of the bare-knuckle mills of the eighteenth century, when prize-fighting phrases were absorbed into conversation. Today, some of these are still readily understood while others have drifted out of fashion.

We understand, for example, what it means to 'come up to scratch' without considering the origin of the phrase. It derives from the 'scratch-line' devised by the man known as the 'Father of Boxing', John Broughton, who gave the sport its first rules in the 1740s following the death of one of his opponents, George Stevenson.

One of his rules introduced the scratch line across the centre of the fighting area. As rounds ended when a man was knocked down, Broughton's idea was that rounds would only begin providing both men could, after a thirty-second rest, place their toes on the scratch line. If they could not 'come up to scratch', then they lost.

The following is a selection of boxing terms:

ACCIDENTAL BUTT

This is a technical term introduced in recent years by the sport's sanctioning bodies. In effect it means an accidental collision of heads, where neither man is deemed to have used the head intentionally. Should the accidental butt cause a cut too severe for the injured man to continue, a 'technical decision' may be given – see below.

BLOCKING

The use of gloves, arms or shoulders to prevent a punch landing on the target area.

BREAK

The command from a referee when boxers are tangled up at close range and will not extricate themselves. When a referee shouts 'Break', boxers are expected to step back before continuing to box.

BUTT

To use the head in a deliberate, intentional movement aimed at the opponent (usually his face). This is one of the most serious offences a boxer can commit. In recent years, American descriptions of a 'butt' have also included accidental head clashes. See 'Accidental Butt'.

CLARET

Prize-fighting term for blood.

CLINCH

When both boxers hold on the inside and do not attempt to punch. A referee will usually order the boxers to break quickly once he establishes that neither is working effectively. It can be used as a chance to rest, or for one boxer to use any physical advantages he has in order to tire his opponent.

COUNTER-PUNCH

A punch thrown as a reply to the opponent's lead. Counter-punching is an accepted method of attack. By drawing the opponent's lead, a good counter-puncher can exploit openings which appear in his opponent's defence when the lead is thrown. Hand speed, a sharp tactical brain and timing are essential for a counter-puncher to be effective.

CROSS

(a) In prize-fighting days a 'cross' meant a fixed fight.

(b) A cross is also a punch, thrown across the target with the 'second' hand. Amateur boxers are taught to follow a lead punch, usually a jab with their leading hand, with a cross from the other fist (i.e. left jab–right cross). The cross punch comes from shoulder level and is therefore usually aimed at the head, or at the lowest the chest.

DISQUALIFICATION

A referee has the power to disqualify a boxer who breaks the rules. He will allow a certain amount of leeway, but in his time almost every referee will have been forced to disqualify a boxer who either refuses to obey instructions, deliberately or repeatedly fouls an opponent, or is guilty of serious misconduct. Under certain commissions, a disqualified boxer will have his pay withheld until he has appeared before a disciplinary hearing, at which point his punishment will be determined.

DRAW

A fight which goes the scheduled distance, at the end of which the scorecard of the referee has both boxers level on points. In fights where three officials' cards determine the outcome, a draw can happen in three ways: (a) if one judge has boxer A in front, one has boxer B in front, and the third judge has them level; (b) if two judges have both boxers level, while the third has one boxer ahead, in which case the majority verdict stands; (c) if all three judges have the fight level.

FEINT

Basically a move which is designed to deceive an opponent into thinking a certain punch is about to be thrown. It's an essential part of a boxer's tool-kit. Boxers who use feints as they move into attacking positions are less likely to get hit on the way in, while those who use the feint as a defensive manoeuvre are less likely to get hit. 'Feinting each other into knots' is a cliche used to describe two boxers who stand in punching range, deceiving each other with slight movements of the body or glove, and consequently cancelling out any attacking moves either of them intends to make.

FIX

A fight in which the outcome is predetermined by either both boxers or an outside party or parties. It happens rarely, and is usually very difficult to prove, although cynics who do not approve of the outcome of a fight will often sneer, without any evidence whatsoever to back up their accusations: 'Ah, that was a fix!'

GATE

The receipts paid at the box office. The 'gate' was originally used in prize-fighting, where even though contests would be held in an open field, a gate would be set up, through which spectators had to pass, either paying with cash or by presenting a ticket which they had bought in advance. The great bare-knuckle fighter of the late eighteenth century, Daniel Mendoza, was one of the first to insist that boxers should work only in front of a paying audience. 'Gate' can also mean the size of the crowd, but more accurately describes the amount of money paid by the public.

GUMSHIELD

Called a mouthpiece in the USA. Pioneered by Britain's great world champion Ted 'Kid' Lewis, it fits over the gums allowing a boxer to bite down on to it and effectively clamp or tighten his jaw. Medical officers of today insist on gumshields being worn, and referees are under instruction to replace them at the earliest opportunity should they fall out.

HAYMAKER
A wild punch, usually thrown round arm in a sweeping motion and in a measure of desperation.

HEEL OF THE GLOVE
To use the bottom of the glove, which has rough edges and can therefore be used to injure an opponent, in a clinch is a serious foul. Similarly, it is an offence to rub an opponent's face with the lace of the glove.

HOLDING
A boxer often holds if he is hurt. Technically, it is a foul, but usually a referee will allow a man to hold for a brief time if his opponent is continuing to work with at least one free hand. Some boxers hold in order to conserve energy, or to disrupt the fighting rhythm of an opponent. Referees are more likely to penalise this kind of holding rapidly, but will often – unofficially – use their discretion if they feel a man is hanging on to allow his head to clear. But while he is holding, he can score no points and therefore will be losing ground on the referee's card.

HOLDING AND HITTING
This is a foul. Part of the skill of boxing is that the punches are aimed at a moving target. If a man is allowed to hold his opponent in a fixed position with one hand and then punch with the other, he is deemed to have an unfair advantage.

HOOK
A punch, most effective when thrown in a short arc rather than from long range, in which the boxer

VETERANS RALLY

The oldest men to win titles in each division, and the age at which they became champion:

Heavyweight: George Foreman (45 years, 10 months, 25 days)
Cruiserweight: James Warring (33 years, 9 months, 11 days)
Light-heavy: Bob Fitzsimmons (40 years, 5 months, 30 days)
Super-middle: Fulgencio Obelmejias (35 years, 5 months, 22 days)
Middle: Roberto Duran (37 years, 8 months, 8 days)
Light-middle: Gianfranco Rosi (38 years, 9 months, 9 days)
Welter: Jack Britton (33 years, 5 months, 3 days)
Light-welter: Saoul Mamby (32 years, 8 months, 19 days)
Lightweight: Claude Noel (33 years, 1 month, 18 days)
Super-feather: Kamel Bou-Ali (31 years, 3 days)
Feather: Eder Jofre (37 years, 1 month, 10 days)
Super-bantam: Daniel Zaragoza (37 years, 5 months, 26 days)
Bantam: Johnny Buff (33 years, 3 months, 11 days)
Super-fly: Santos Laciar (28 years, 3 months, 16 days)
Flyweight: Dado Marino (33 years, 11 months, 6 days)
Light-flyweight: Luis Estaba (34 years, 1 month)
Straw-weight: Samuth Sithnaruepol (28 years, 10 months, 7 days)

BABY BOOMERS

The ages at which the game's youngest champions were crowned:

Heavyweight: Mike Tyson (20 years, 4 months, 22 days)
Cruiserweight: Carlos DeLeon (21 years, 6 months, 20 days)
Light-heavy: Michael Moorer (21 years, 21 days)
Super-middle: Darrin Van Horn (22 years, 8 months, 11 days)
Middle: Al McCoy (19 years, 5 months, 14 days)
Light-middle: Darrin Van Horn (20 years, 4 months, 28 days)
Welter: Pipino Cuevas (18 years, 6 months, 20 days)
Light-welter: Wilfred Benitez (17 years, 5 months, 24 days)
Lightweight: Edwin Rosario (20 years, 1 month, 17 days)
Super-feather: Ben Villaflor (19 years, 5 months, 15 days)
Feather: Tony Canzoneri (18 years, 11 months, 18 days)
Super-bantam: Julio Gervacio (20 years, 1 month, 11 days)
Bantam: Teddy Baldock (18 years, 11 months, 15 days)
Super-fly: Cesar Polanco (18 years, 2 months, 17 days)
Flyweight: Joe Symonds (19 years, 4 months, 18 days)
Light-flyweight: Netrnoi Vorasingh (19 years, 14 days)
Straw-weight: Hiroki Ioka (18 years, 9 months, 10 days)

turns his wrist at the point of impact. The longer the punch, the less likely it is to be controlled or to carry full power.

KIDNEY PUNCH

An extremely dangerous foul, thrown around the side to the kidney area on the back.

KNOCKOUT

When a man is floored by a punch and cannot rise before the referee counts to ten. This can be a thorny issue for boxing authorities. Technically, the British Board of Control does not recognise the term. To stay within British law, boxing must be a 'contest' rather than a fight. Therefore when a referee either counts a man out or stops the contest to save him taking punishment, the round in which the fight ends is scored with a maximum to the winner, and nil to the loser. The scoring system is devised so that a man cannot score a knockout and yet lose on points. In this way, points will always officially decide a contest.

Until recently, Americans tended to follow the practice instituted by Nat Fleischer in his *Ring Record Book* and record any inside-the-distance ending as a knockout even if, for example, the loser might have been leading widely on points when he sustained a cut eye. This often gave a misleading impression of both a boxer's punching power and ability to take a punch. Howard Winstone, the brilliant Welsh featherweight of the 1960s, was so skilful that he used to bamboozle opponents into exhaustion until the referee would be forced to rescue the outclassed loser, yet he never scored a single countout in his sixty-seven fights. According to the Americans, however, he had twenty-seven 'knockouts'. Conversely, former world middleweight champion Alan Minter is shown as having suffered eight 'knockout' defeats, suggesting that he had a glass jaw, whereas in fact seven of those were cut eye losses.

Modern American record books now differentiate between the terms KO and TKO, or technical knockout, which is the equivalent of the British 'referee stopped fight'. A recent refinement in British boxing has introduced the term 'technical countout' to cover the situation where the referee abandons the contest without completing the ten count, when it is obvious that the loser is beaten or needs immediate medical attention. Previously, such an ending would have been recorded as 'rsf' rather than KO, thus depriving the winner of the credit due him for scoring the knockout.

LOW BLOW

Any punch which lands below the imaginary line across the top of the hips. The height of a boxer's trunks or protector is irrelevant when determining a low punch, but it is up to the referee to lower the trunks or protector of a boxer who wears them above the line of the hips.

MARK

The pit of the chest between the ribcage, sometimes called the 'Solar Plexus'. Bob Fitzsimmons knocked out James J. Corbett with something that one pretentious writer labelled the 'Solar Plexus punch'. The name was picked up by others and repeated as if Fitzsimmons had done something revolutionary. He scoffed at the suggestion. All he had done, as his wife Rose had yelled at him to do from ringside, was hit Corbett 'in the slats'.

MILLING ON THE RETREAT

A prize-fighting term, used to describe the technique of fighting when moving backwards. It is difficult to fight effectively off the back foot, but good fighters can use the tactic to steal points while waiting for the right moment to counter-attack.

MUFFLERS

These were early gloves or bandages used in the prize-fighting academies of the eighteenth and nineteenth centuries. Society gentlemen were encouraged to box rather than settle their arguments with either sword or pistol, but while learning the art they attempted to avoid the pain and inconvenience of bruises or cuts by using mufflers. These were introduced by John Broughton in his school off what is now Oxford Street in London in the 1740s.

NEUTRAL CORNER

Either of the corners which are not used by the boxer or his seconds. It is to a neutral corner that a boxer must go when he scores a knockdown, This rule was introduced in the 1920s to foil men like Jack Dempsey, who would stand over an opponent until he had raised both gloves off the canvas and then attack again while he was effectively still defenceless. Dempsey's failure to go to a neutral corner in his rematch with Gene Tunney in 1927 caused the famous 'Long Count' imposed by referee Dave Barry. Tunney was on the floor for fourteen seconds, but Barry only reached the count of nine because Dempsey forgot the new rule. 'What the hell is a neutral corner?' he said in disgust afterwards.

NOBBINS

Money tossed into the ring at the end of an especially good contest by appreciative spectators, a practice which, regrettably, has almost died out. The word derives from the practice of fairground booth owners to 'menace' money from spectators. The public was usually allowed to watch early bouts free, but as the better boxers appeared, then undercard fighters would pass among the crowd with a hat, into which it was expected the customers would drop a coin or two. Those who refused ran the risk of being cracked 'on the nob', which was an old term for the skull.

NO CONTEST

A fight which is effectively cancelled by the referee because of the lack of effort of the boxers involved. It has also been used recently in cases where a boxer wins a fight, but then fails a drug test.

NO DECISION

Originally this term was used to describe bouts which lasted the 'prescribed distance' in New York State after the introduction of the Frawley Law in 1911. The law stated that boxing contests should be exhibitions and therefore no decision could be given as to the winner. Whereas when a man was knocked out it was obvious who was the winner, in which case the law turned a blind eye, in distance fights it was left to popular opinion to determine who was the better man. Newspaper reporters working at ringside usually gave their verdict, and bets were settled on the basis of their opinions. This situation lasted into the 1920s. Modern researchers are only now trawling through old newspapers in an effort to trace who actually won the No Decision bouts on the records of the famous fighters of the time.

In the modern era a No Decision verdict has been used in circumstances whereby a fight is abandoned through no fault of either boxer (for example, a riot in the crowd, a power failure or even the collapse of the ring!).

PULLING A PUNCH

The art of drawing back a punch at the point of impact. This renders the blow harmless. It takes a practised eye to identify it from ringside if the boxer using it is experienced. It was often used in boxing booth contests between men who would be expected to fight each other every night: their term for such encounters was a 'gee fight'.

PUNCH ON THE BREAK

An old pro's trick. When a referee calls 'break' both boxers should take a step back without throwing a punch. But it is not uncommon for a boxer to try a sneak shot just as he steps back, before he has completed the movement. This is a foul. It can be damaging if the opponent has relaxed his defence. Evander Holyfield was disqualified for this offence in the 1984 Olympic semi-final.

RABBIT PUNCH

A dangerous punch and a serious foul. The punch is named after the chop to the back of the neck which is the traditional country method of killing a rabbit. It can cause serious damage to humans too! Not enough referees clamp down on it.

REFEREE

The 'third man' in the ring, whose job it is to control the fight and ensure that the boxers stay within the rules. In early gloved contests at the National Sporting Club in London, where silence was observed during rounds, referees would follow the old prize-fighting tradition and sit outside the ring. Only if the boxers failed to follow his instructions would he enter the ring.

SLAP

A punch which lands with the open glove. It should not be counted as a scoring punch. Often slaps make more noise than a legitimate blow, which to the uninitiated sounds impressive, but which actually does little harm.

SLIP

When a fighter falls to the ground without receiving a punch. This is not a knockdown but a referee will normally order the standing boxer to step back while the fallen boxer rises. Before action resumes, the referee should check the boxer's condition and wipe his gloves free of any dust or debris from the canvas.

SLIPPING (PUNCHES)

Movement of the head or shoulders, without backward foot movement, to avoid a punch. Punches can be 'slipped' on the way forward, but usually backward movement will make them fall short.

SOLAR PLEXUS – See 'Mark'.

SOUTHPAW

The orthodox way to box is with the left foot and left hand leading. This is considered the most effective way for a right-handed boxer to operate, although some left-handed fighters prefer to box from an orthodox stance. However, many right-handed youngsters who begin to box automatically put their right side forward in what is known as the southpaw stance. Most coaches will turn them around. Traditional coaches disliked boxers, left-handed or right-handed, to fight southpaw. There was an old saying that 'southpaws should be drowned at birth'. Today, coaches take a more relaxed view, and southpaws seem to be increasing in number by the year.

The term is derived from baseball, where the pitcher traditionally throws from east to west. This way, as most games were played in the afternoon, pitchers were not pitching out of the sun. In the northern hemisphere, right-handed pitchers therefore throw with their throwing arm to the north, left-handers to the south.

SPARRING
Boxing in the gym. A valuable training procedure whereby moves and technical skills can be fine-tuned or taught. It should not be competitive, but too often is.

SPLIT DECISION
The term used when two of the three scoring officials vote for the same man and the third scores the fight to his opponent. This is not to be confused with a majority decision, when two of the three judges vote for a draw.

SWALLOW
Derogatory term used to describe a boxer who has given in without showing sufficient courage.

TECHNICAL DECISION

This is a rule used by some governing bodies when a fight ends because of an injury. The bout goes to the scorecards, which are totalled. The boxer who is ahead on points at the time of the stoppage is awarded a Technical Decision – in effect, a technical points win.

TECHNICAL DRAW

This is used to describe a contest which ends because of an injury caused by an accidental foul before a predetermined number of rounds has been completed. In 1997, the most powerful sanctioning bodies met and ironed out a uniform set of rules for world title fights, which set the limit at four rounds. A more complicated variation of this rule was also used by some authorities in order to prevent a man winning by a foul. If, for example, a butt opened a slight cut on an opponent, but not one serious enough to curtail the contest, then the boxer who committed the butt could not win the contest in the event of that injury worsening at a later stage, even if it worsened as a result of legal blows. If that happened, and the boxer who committed the foul was ahead on the scorecards, a technical draw would be ruled. If the boxer who committed the foul was behind on the cards, then the injured boxer would win a technical decision. See 'Technical Decision'.

THROWING IN THE TOWEL

In some countries, especially in continental Europe, a boxer's seconds may throw a towel into the ring as a signal to the referee that they wish to retire their man. The gesture is not formally recognised in Britain, where the decision to stop a fight is the referee's: if he feels the time is not right to end the fight, he will simply throw or kick the towel out again.

BOXING IN PRINT

The first known newspaper report of a prize-fight appeared in the *Protestant Mercury* in January 1681, on 'a match of boxing before His Grace, the Duke of Albemarle, between the Duke's footman and a butcher.' The butcher won.

The earliest known book on boxing is *A Treatise Upon The Useful Science Of Defence*, by one Capt. Godfrey. It was published in 1747. The first boxing magazine was *Boxing Reviewed*, published by Thomas Fewtrell in 1790.

FIRST SET OF RULES

These were drawn up by Jack Broughton in 1743, following the death two years earlier of one of his opponents, George Stevenson. The affair affected Broughton so deeply that he campaigned for the introduction of rules in hopes of reducing the likelihood of tragedy in the ring. His Rules governed the sport for almost 100 years, until the introduction of the London Prize Ring Rules in 1838.

END OF AN ERA

On 7 February 1882, John L. Sullivan beat Paddy Ryan in nine rounds to become the last bare-knuckle heavyweight champion. On 8 July 1889 he stopped Jake Kilrain in seventy-five rounds in the last bare-knuckle title fight, and on 7 September 1892 he lost to James J. Corbett in twenty-one rounds in the first gloved heavyweight title fight.

BOXING ON SCREEN

Bob Fitzsimmons' fourteenth round knockout of James J. Corbett in Carson City, New Jersey, on 17 March 1897 was the first championship fight to be filmed, and Fitzsimmons' victory made him the first English-born world heavyweight champion.

The first 'fight' to be filmed was an exhibition between Corbett and Peter Courtney over six rounds at Edison Laboratories, Llewellyn, New Jersey in 1897. Jack Johnson's knockout of Ben Taylor at the Cosmopolitan Gymnasium, Plymouth on 31 July 1908 was the first British fight to be filmed.

LONDON HOSTS A FIRST

The world heavyweight title was contested outside America for the first time when Tommy Burns beat Gunner Moir at the National Sporting Club, London on 2 December 1907. Burns, a real globe-trotter, also took part in the first heavyweight title fights in Ireland, France and Australia.

BLACK BREAKTHROUGH

Jack Johnson, an ex-docker from Galveston, Texas, became the first black heavyweight champion when he stopped Tommy Burns in Sydney on 26 December 1908. His victory sparked race riots and lynchings across America, and inspired writer Jack London – a ringside reporter at the fight – to launch the infamous campaign to find a Great White Hope to dethrone him.

The twenty boxers featured here – in strictly alphabetical order – are not necessarily the best in their profession, although the chances are that most of them would feature in that list too. A few, like Julio Cesar Chavez, Roberto Duran, Arturo Gatti and even Mike Tyson, are past their prime, but still command a place in this particular top twenty because the men you will meet here are the entertainers, the crowd-pleasers, the performers you simply have to watch when their fights are on TV.

Tracking some of them down might be difficult, as even brilliant little champions like Ricardo Lopez do not get anything like the air time afforded to half-competent heavyweights, but it's worth trawling the satellite channels to find them. The German DSF channel is particularly rewarding, and is often the only chance to see regular world-class boxing from around the world. So learn the names and watch out for them: we guarantee you won't be disappointed when you see them in action.

LUIS RAMON CAMPAS

Status: *IBF light-middleweight champion.* **Born**: *5 August 1971, Navojoa, Mexico.*

The heavy-fisted Campas, whose nickname is 'Yory Boy', was just past his sixteenth birthday when he made his pro start, and since then he has matured into a fearsome puncher who has knocked out fifty-nine opponents in compiling a record of 69–2. Both his losses came in world title bids, the first in an up-and-down thriller against Felix Trinidad for the IBF welterweight title in 1994 and the other a stoppage loss to Mexican rival Jose Luis Lopez for the WBO belt.

He moved up to light-middleweight in 1996, and his ten-year quest for a title ended in December 1997 when he battered IBF champion Raul Marquez to defeat in eight rounds, the Texan's first loss in twenty-nine fights. When he returned from Atlantic City with the title, the people of Navojoa lined the streets to welcome him, his wife Mabel and son Ramon, known as Yorito.

Campos, the youngest of a railroad worker's three children, was introduced to the sport at eleven by his elder brother, who used to beat him up so badly that Yory would finish up chasing him with a rock. At fifteen, he left Navojoa for Tijuana, one of Mexico's busiest boxing centres, where his explosive punching made him a major attraction. He knocked out his first thirteen foes, six of them in the first round and three in the second, before going the distance for the first time.

After winning and defending the Mexican title, he made the big breakthrough in Las Vegas by beating world-ranked Roger Turner for the North American title, and since then has fought as often in America as in his native country. He developed a ring entrance that Naseem Hamed might envy, being preceded into the ring by a dancing, chanting shaman (an Indian holy man) wearing a deer's head and brandishing feathers, while Campas himself wore a crest of feathers presented to him in Tijuana by a Mexican welterweight favourite from the 1960s, Gaspar Ortega.

'The head-dress was a source of pride for me, and the dancing and chanting was to show a little bit of my roots, as homage to the place I grew up and which I still call home', he explained. He dropped the act after failing in his second world title bid, but promised to revive it if he ever became champion. Maybe Campas won't be champion for long, but at least the shaman is guaranteed one more night's work.

JULIO CESAR CHAVEZ

Status: *Former world champion at three weights.*
Born: *12 July 1962, Ciudad Obregon, Mexico*

The fire burns low these days, as age and the rigours of a 103-fight career take their toll, but there just might be another world title for the fabulous Mexican before he finally quits. He boxed a draw with his young compatriot Miguel Angel Gonzalez in March 1998 for the vacant WBC light-welterweight title, and victory in the obligatory rematch would cement Chavez' claim to be regarded as his country's best-ever fighter.

He already holds the record for title fights – thirty-one wins and two draws in thirty-five championship contests – and compiled that staggering total across four weight divisions and twelve years. Chavez turned pro as a seventeen-year-old in 1980, and won his first world title – the WBC super-featherweight belt – in his forty-fourth undefeated fight in 1984. His methodical, almost robotic style was built around an unhurried aggression, alternating crippling body shots with short hooks to the head. He was never flustered or ruffled in the ring, and as he swept aside eight super-featherweight challengers before stepping up to take the WBA and WBC lightweight titles in 1987 and 1988, he seemed truly unbeatable.

Increasing weight forced him up a division, and he relinquished his lightweight belts on becoming a triple champion by taking the WBC light-welterweight title from Roger Mayweather. The boxing world saw the best of Chavez as a light-welter (10 st), as he scored eighteen championship victories against two losses. In 1990, he added the IBF title with an unforgettable stoppage of the dazzling, unbeaten former Olympic champion Meldrick Taylor, who was in an unassailable points lead when Chavez stopped him with just two seconds remaining in the twelfth and final round.

Julio Caesar Chavez (left) finds the youth and speed of Oscar De La Hoya too hot to handle in their 1996 title fight

Three years later he made an audacious bid for a fourth title against yet another former Olympic winner, Pernell Whitaker, who held the WBC welterweight belt. They met in San Antonio, Texas in front of a huge and predominantly Mexican crowd, whose passionate support may have swayed

the judges into giving Chavez a draw he did not deserve. It was the first sign of decay, and defeat finally came in his ninety-first contest when the unsung American Frankie Randall took his light-welterweight title. Chavez won it back in a rematch, and defended it a further four times before Oscar De La Hoya cut him up in four rounds in a clash of the generations, Old Mexico against the new California–Mexican.

Everything seemed to go wrong at once for Chavez, a national idol at whose home fans would queue just to glimpse the champion. Shortly after the De La Hoya loss, his wife divorced him amid bitter accusations of domestic violence, drinking and drug-taking, and recurring injuries hampered his comeback plans. But whatever he does in the future, his astonishing record guarantees him a place with the sport's legends.

OSCAR DE LA HOYA

Status: *WBC welterweight champion, who has held titles at four weights.* **Born:** *4 February 1973, Los Angeles*

If you are looking for the perfect fighter, look no further. De La Hoya is the man with everything: talent enough to win an Olympic gold medal and four world titles by the age of twenty-four, and the kind of dark good looks that make him the most marketable star in the sport. He has won fifteen title fights at weights from super-feather to welter, has beaten ten sometime world champions, and is poised to win a fifth title – at light-middle – in 1998.

A third-generation professional, he began boxing aged six and won 223 of 228 amateur fights, culminating in the 1992 Olympic gold at lightweight. He was America's only boxing winner, and when the nation learned that he had just lost his mother from cancer, he became everybody's favourite son. The game's moneymen recognised the extent of his appeal, across the communities as well as the sexes, since he drew his following as much from middle-class white America as from the Latin quarters in Los Angeles. The result was a fabulous contract, the richest ever offered to a fledgling pro, which made him a millionaire even before he won the WBO super-featherweight title in only his twelfth outing.

There is a ruthless streak behind the 'Pretty Boy' facade, though, as he demonstrated by sacking his managers as soon as he had become champion, and then later in his career by dumping the respected trainer Emanuel Steward when he felt he was not enjoying Steward's undivided attention.

He vacated the super-feather title in June 1994 to win the WBO lightweight belt, and added the IBF's version in May 1995 with a brilliant two-rounds stoppage of Rafael Ruelas. At the time he was the WBO's highest-profile representative, and they were hugely flattered when he opted to relinquish the IBF belt but keep theirs. In June 1996 he went up against his boyhood idol, Julio Cesar Chavez, with whom he had sparred prior to the Olympic Games, and took the Mexican's WBC light-welterweight title with a bloody defeat in four rounds on an emotional evening at Caesars Palace, Las Vegas.

He defended it only once, inflicting the first defeat in forty-two fights on Miguel Angel Gonzalez, and then took a controversial verdict over WBC welterweight king, Pernell Whitaker, to claim his fourth championship. De La Hoya's boxing brain and dazzling combination punching will almost certainly push his ring earnings above $100m, and the couple of knockdowns he suffered in early fights do not seem to indicate any vulnerability. He's as close to flawless as a fighter can get.

ROBERTO DURAN

Status: *Former champion at four weights.* **Born:** *16 June 1951, Guarare, Panama*

Forget George Foreman: Roberto Duran is the true marvel of the ages. George has only appeared sporadically over the last four years, and then always against hand-picked opposition, but the irrepressible Duran, a pro at fifteen, is still a thorough-going professional fighter, working hard at his trade and capable of trouncing youngsters half his age. It was typical of the man for whom the adjective 'swashbuckling' might have been coined that he celebrated his 100th win not over some obliging fall-guy but against Jorge Castro, one of the toughest middleweight champions of recent years, who had outpointed Duran a few months previously.

Duran loves boxing so much that it is near-impossible to imagine him in retirement, and he clearly has the same problem himself. It would be easier for him to ride gracefully into the sunset if he was routinely beaten up by inferior rivals, but even in his late forties he loses only to the best, and gives them all hell. That is the only way he knows how to fight, or to live: he has made and squandered fortunes, but there has always been another big-money match around the corner to make him solvent again.

Roberto Duran, the supreme showman

Nobody seriously disputes that he was the finest lightweight in history, with a record-equalling twelve defences of the championship he clawed away from Scotland's Ken Buchanan in thirteen savage rounds in Madison Square Garden in 1972. The only real argument is about his placing in the all-time, pound-for-pound top ten, where many would rank him on a par with Muhammad Ali and Sugar Ray Robinson.

He won his second title, at welterweight, from Ray Leonard and then sullied his reputation by quitting in the rematch. But forgiveness came when he ripped the WBA light-middleweight title from the unbeaten Davey Moore and then defied Marvin Hagler for fifteen marvellous rounds in a cheeky bid for the middleweight title. Thomas Hearns flattened him in two rounds next time out, the worst defeat of his career, but in 1989 the old warhorse picked up his fourth title (which he never lost in the ring), when he outsmarted the fearsome Iran Barkley for the WBC middleweight title.

He has had other chances since then and failed, but a fighter as glamorous as Duran will never be short of opportunities. Some day soon, of course, even his engine must wear out, but until then the veteran Panamanian will continue to thrill audiences around the world. He is the supreme showman, the greatest fighter of his time – or maybe even of all time.

LUISITO ESPINOSA

Status: *WBC featherweight and former WBA bantamweight champion.* **Born:** *26 June 1967, Manila, Philippines*

When you are born one of fourteen children in the wrong part of Manila, as Luisito Espinosa was, you learn early how to look after yourself. He was sparring by the time he was seven, sharpening his power and timing by punching a sackful of sand. It was a predictable course for his life to take, since his father Dio had been a good pro who once went the distance with former two-weights world champion Fighting Harada of Japan, while his uncle Leo Espinosa was outpointed in world flyweight title challenges against Yoshio Shirai and Pascual Perez and then knocked out by Raton Macias for the NBA bantamweight belt, between 1954–6.

Luisito had only three amateur bouts before turning pro aged sixteen in May 1984. The competition was tough at his weight, but the tall youngster with the mean left hook gradually fought his way through the pack until, in October 1989, he was selected as a safe opponent for one of Thailand's hottest attractions, WBA bantamweight champion Khaokor Galaxy. The Thai was in his second spell as champion, but Espinosa sensationally disposed of him in the opening round.

He went on to retain the title three times, twice in Thailand and once in front of his home fans in Manila, before Venezuelan challenger Israel Contreras knocked him out in five rounds in Manila. It took him time to rebuild from that setback, and in the meantime he moved up to featherweight – more the natural division for someone of his 5ft 8ins – and changed management. Joe Kozumi, a well-respected and equally well-connected boxing writer and promoter, took his career in hand in 1995 and within the year had made him a double champion. Espinosa outpointed Manuel Medina to win the

WBC belt in December 1995 and has been a busy champion since then, with five defences, four of them inside the distance, including a stunning knockout of former champion Alejandro Gonzalez of Mexico. He signed a promotional deal with British promoter Frank Warren in 1998, and will be seen in action before facing WBO champion Naseem Hamed in an eagerly-awaited championship unification match. His cracking left jab and powerful hooks have brought him (by the start of 1998) forty-two wins in forty-nine fights, and he could be the toughest opponent yet for Hamed.

ARTURO GATTI

Status: *Former IBF super-featherweight champion.* **Born:** *15 April 1972, Montreal, Canada*

A shattering knockout by Angel Manfredy early in 1998 has probably marked the end of Gatti's championship aspirations, but he remains a thrilling performer who has never been in a dull fight. His nickname, 'Thunder', is apt, as the New Jersey-based Canadian slugger has blown away twenty-four of his thirty-one opponents, fourteen of them inside a round.

His brother Joe, seven years his senior, is a pro super-middleweight who once fought Terry Norris for the WBC light-middleweight title, being kayoed in the opening round. Arturo followed him into the sport, at the prompting of his boxing-mad father Giovanni, and was an instant success with three Canadian Golden Gloves titles before turning pro in June 1991. The brothers moved to New Jersey to join the Duva family's Main Events team, since there is little pro boxing in Canada, and the move certainly paid off for Arturo.

His all-action style quickly made him a crowd favourite in Atlantic City and New York, and he won the United States title in his seventeenth fight when, typically, he stopped Pete Talliafero in the first round. Two defences of that belt moved him into a challenge for Tracy Harris Patterson's WBC championship, which Gatti won in December 1995 in a blistering twelve-rounder which stole the Madison Square Garden show from the chief attraction, Oscar De La Hoya.

He was back three months later to retain the title against Wilson Rodriguez in a punch-up even more demanding than the Patterson match. Gatti was floored in the second round and cut around both eyes before rallying to stop his man in the sixth. In a rematch with Patterson he won a clear decision in a fight which was low-key by his standards – yet the ringside punch-count showed that he threw over 1,000 in the twelve rounds.

Arturo Gatti (left) wins an epic battle against Gabriel Ruelas in 1997

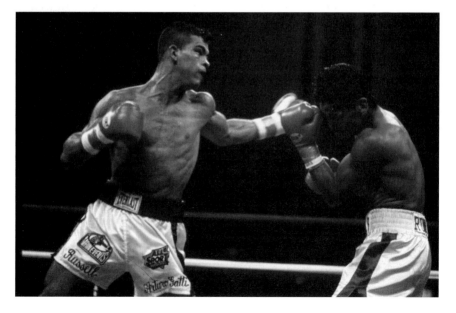

His latest victory, a one-punch, five rounds knockout of former WBC boss Gabriel Ruelas on the Lennox Lewis v Andrew Golota bill in October 1997, was the most thrilling of all, with Gatti on the very brink of being stopped before salvaging the fight with a single left hook.

Increasing weight forced him to relinquish the title and move up to lightweight, but the beating he took from Manfredy on his debut there will be hard to come back from. Gatti is aware of the dangers of his style. 'Fighters who take those kind of punches don't last too long', he acknowledges.

NASEEM HAMED

Status: *WBO and former undefeated IBF featherweight champion.* **Born:** *12 February 1974, Sheffield*

The self-styled Prince is one of those rare athletes who have transcended their sport to become known on a wider stage. His outrageous posturing and bragging have made him a national figure, and even those with no particular interest in boxing watch his fights – if only in the hope of seeing him humbled. They may have to wait some time for that to happen, though, as there are few legitimate challengers left for an extraordinary, unique performer whose style defies classification.

He is a genuine original. His hands-dangling stance echoes Muhammad Ali, but he hits with proportionately far greater power than Ali and has the added edge of being equally at home in an orthodox or southpaw (leading with the right) stance. There are refinements Ali never thought of, such as staring at an opponent's feet while smacking an accurate jab into his face, but after the scare he had against Kevin Kelley on his American debut in December 1997, when he had to come off the floor three times to win, Hamed's future performances may be a little more subdued.

The story of his introduction to boxing as a seven-year-old has often been told, with embellishments from his career-long trainer Brendan Ingle, an Irish ex-middleweight to whose gym Hamed's Yemeni-born father brought him to learn the basics of self-defence. Ingle is a wonderful teacher with an eye for natural talent, and he recognised something special in the precocious youngster. Hamed became the gym mascot, sparring with seasoned pros like Herol Graham and Brian Anderson before he was even a teenager.

There was talk of him competing for the Yemen in the 1992 Olympics, but instead he turned pro with Ingle and won the European bantamweight title in only his twelfth fight. He added the WBC International super-bantam title in his next fight, defending it five times before crushing Steve Robinson for the WBO featherweight title. His reputation grew as he destroyed four challengers in eight months before taking the IBF belt from Tom Johnson, in February 1997.

Boxing politics forced him to relinquish the IBF belt after only one defence, but he continued to defend his WBO belt regularly and, with that sensational win over Kevin Kelley, he has now crashed the American market as well. His awesome power was in evidence in April 1998, when he destroyed Wilfredo Vasquez in seven rounds. Vasquez, the undefeated WBA champion, had relinquished the title in order to take the Hamed fight. He is not even in his prime yet, and his potential is awesome; when he talks of winning at least two more world titles, it is a plain statement of intent rather than an empty boast.

BERNARD HOPKINS

Status: *IBF middleweight champion.* **Born:** *15 January 1965, Philadelphia*

Anyone who calls himself 'The Executioner' and enters the ring in a headsman's hood, preceded by attendants carrying an axe, had better be able to fight. Luckily for Bernard Hopkins, he can: in fact, at thirty-three he is maturing into the best the middleweight division has seen since the fearsome Marvin Hagler was in his prime in the mid-1980s. Hopkins, who has made seven defences of the IBF belt he won at the third attempt in December 1994, comes from the classic background of the American boxer: crime and the ghetto. He was raised in the notorious 'housing projects' in the Germantown area of Philadelphia, and served nearly five years in Graterford Prison, Pennsylvania for armed robbery.

It was a tough time, but he acknowledges now that the experience 'saved his life'. He has not forgotten the men he left behind bars, and still returns regularly to Graterford to spar with the jail's toughest inmates. 'There are 3,000 guys in here, and I know 2,000 of them', he says. 'They see me as someone who made it, and I'm bringing them hope that they can make it too.'

He turned pro late, at twenty-four, without any amateur pedigree, and lost his debut. But he learned quickly and well, and was not beaten again for almost five years. He developed a methodical, unhurried style built around accurate body punching, but could also seize the openings however soon they presented themselves: he has thirteen first-round knockouts on his record.

There was no disgrace about his next defeat, as the unbeatable Roy Jones outscored him in a hard twelve-rounder for the vacant IBF title. When Jones eventually moved up to super-middle, Hopkins was paired with Segundo Mercado for the vacant title. It proved a real test of character, as he had to come off the floor twice to earn a draw and a rematch. This time, he finally made it with a seventh-round stoppage, and has been a busy champion since then with six of his seven defences won inside schedule. He has grow in status as champion, and while he remains a shade one-paced and can sometimes be outboxed, his formidable combination of patience and power usually carries him through.

Given his hometown's tradition of great middleweights, he is rightly proud of being the city's first champion in the division. (Joey Giardello, normally accorded that honour, was actually a transplanted New Yorker.)

MARK JOHNSON

Status: *IBF flyweight champion.* **Born:** *13 August 1971, Washington DC*

Mark 'Too Sharp' Johnson is unlikely to be added to the depressingly long list of ex-fighters who finish up with nothing. He already co-owns (with his wife) two barber shops and a health club in Washington, and plans to qualify as a dental technician when he retires. He was only a year away from completing the course when he turned pro in February 1990, and, despite being an exciting knockout puncher, he is well aware that he will need something to fall back on when his career is over, since flyweights do not make heavyweight money, however gifted they may be. 'Heavyweights cheat the fans', Johnson says. 'We don't – we give them value for money.'

The species was virtually extinct in America between, roughly, 1950 and 1980, and when Johnson knocked out Francisco Tejedor in the first round for the vacant IBF title in May 1996, he became only the third American flyweight king since Midget Wolgast in 1931. He is also his country's first black flyweight champion, the division usually being dominated by Latins and Orientals.

A strong and aggressive southpaw, Johnson was an outstanding amateur who won the national Golden Gloves in 1989 and lost only five of 130 contests. Unfortunately, one of the losses was when it mattered most, in an Olympic trial against Eric Griffin, so Griffin went to the Games and Johnson turned pro. He was not an overnight sensation: defeat came in only his second fight which, curiously, took place in Belfast when Richie Wenton – later to become British super-bantam champion – outpointed him in a four-rounder. He has never lost since.

The absence of flyweight competition in Washington meant that he had to move West to California, where he practised his trade against a succession of tough Mexicans (including former WBO champion Alberto Jiminez) in front of hard-to-please crowds in the Los Angeles arenas.

They soon warmed to his hard-punching style, and Johnson had no qualms about adapting his natural approach, that of a fleet-footed punch placer, in order to become more aggressive and crowd-pleasing. 'I'm prepared to take one or two punches to make it a better fight for the fans', he acknowledges. He didn't have to in his latest defence, against American namesake Arthur Johnson: that was all over in exactly seventy-one seconds, giving him his third quick win in five defences.

ROY JONES

Status: *Former undefeated IBF middle and super-middleweight champion, and former WBC light-heavyweight champion.* **Born:** *16 January 1969, Pensacola, Florida*

If Roy Jones's commitment matched his talent, he would deservedly be ranked as the world's no. 1 at any weight. But there are worrying signs that, at twenty-nine, he is letting his career slip past – not least his bizarre decision to play in a semi-pro basketball match on the afternoon of a world title defence against Eric Lucas, which showed a serious lack of respect for his sport as well as his opponent. He has already won titles at three weights, and only a temperamental lapse which earned him disqualification in a WBC light-heavyweight defence for hitting Montell Griffin while Griffin was taking a count mars his perfect record.

He blitzed Griffin inside a round in the rematch in August 1997, but since then ... nothing. He gave up the light-heavyweight belt in November, and demanded $6m to skip the cruiserweight class and face former heavyweight champion Buster

Douglas, yet when the match was made he announced that his father disapproved so he was withdrawing.

His father's influence has always been powerful, but not always beneficial. Roy Sr was a pro middleweight who once fought Marvin Hagler, and he started his son boxing when the boy was seven, training him with an intensity which often passed over into cruelty. Roy Jr was a good learner, and became an American national hero when, in the final of the Seoul Olympics, he was victim of the worst decision in Olympic boxing's scandal-ridden history. He turned pro on a wave of public sympathy, but, with his ultra-cautious father making the decisions, his career stagnated.

Roy Jones (left) made it look easy as he outclassed James Toney for the IBF super-middleweight title

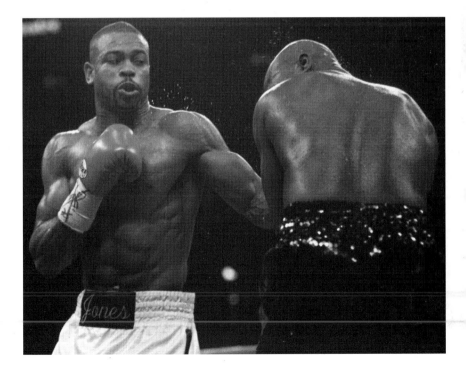

Jones eventually took over his own management, with immediate results. He beat Bernard Hopkins for the vacant IBF middleweight title in 1993, defended it once and then stepped up to super-middle to outclass the intimidating James Toney.

After five impressive defences, he relinquished the title to pursue the light-heavyweight championship. He beat Mike McCallum for the so-called 'interim' WBC title in November 1996, and in February 1997 the WBC stripped champion Fabrice Tiozzo and installed Jones. He had a short reign, losing to Griffin on disqualification, but reclaimed it in sensational style with a first-round knockout in August 1997.

He is supremely gifted in terms of technique, but his destiny now lies in his own hands. He can be one of the greats, or one of the great might-have-beens.

LENNOX LEWIS

Status: *Two-time WBC heavyweight champion.*
Born: *2 September 1965, London*

Lennox Lewis has already made history by becoming the first British-born heavyweight to claim a share of the world title since Bob Fitzsimmons was knocked out by James J. Jeffries in 1899, and there is every chance that he can go all the way and earn undisputed recognition, or as close as anyone can come to that status in these muddled times. Lewis has always had a serene confidence in his destiny, and that never wavered, even when Oliver McCall beat him in two rounds in 1994 to take his WBC belt and inflict his only professional defeat.

The big man is finally coming to his prime, as his latest trainer Emanuel Steward fits the last pieces of the jigsaw in place. It has been a long process, stretching back to 1988 when Lewis, boxing for Canada, stopped Riddick Bowe to win the Olympic super-heavyweight gold medal. (He had joined his mother in Canada at an early age, and did all his boxing there.) He could have had his pick of big-time American managers, but opted instead to come home to London and signed with the hitherto-obscure Frank Maloney. His reasoning was that in America he would be simply another promising young hopeful, but in Britain and Europe, where the talent pool is shallower, he would quickly become a superstar.

It was a shrewd decision, as he soon acquired the European, British and Commonwealth titles. He became WBC champ by default, when his old amateur rival Bowe refused to defend against him. Lewis had stopped Donovan 'Razor' Ruddock in a final eliminator in October 1992, and on the basis of that result he was awarded the vacant title. He learned of his coronation while lounging on a beach in Jamaica, which was really doing it the easy way.

He retained the belt three times before McCall shocked him, and it took three long, patience-testing years to be given a second chance. When it came, by coincidence McCall was in the other corner again, to contest the title vacated by Mike Tyson. It proved the strangest fight in championship history, as poor McCall, ravaged by drugs, suffered a mental collapse and was led weeping from the ring in the fifth round. A disqualification win over a reluctant Henry Akinwande did little to bolster Lewis's reputation, but his one-round demolition of the fearsome

Andrew Golota in October 1997 was the finest result ever achieved in America by a British heavyweight.

It showed Lewis at his best, employing a thudding left jab and following with chilling rights as, boxing with icy self-assurance, he wrecked the man who had ended Bowe's career. The theory is that Lewis tends to be a lazy fighter who comes down to his opponent's level, but conversely can rise to a challenge. His biggest challenges await, but neither Evander Holyfield nor Tyson have shown any eagerness to face him. Maybe, in the end, we'll just have to take Lewis on trust as the best heavyweight of his generation.

Lennox Lewis (left) destroys Andrew Golota in a career-best performance

RICARDO LOPEZ

Status: *WBC and former undefeated WBO straw-weight champion.* **Born:** *25 July 1966, Mexico City*

If Ricardo 'Finito' Lopez had the good fortune to be at the other end of boxing's weight spectrum, he would be talked of with the awe reserved for names like Ali, Louis and Marciano. The Mexican veteran has held the WBC straw-weight (105 lbs) title since November 1990, making him the sport's longest-serving champion, and only four men have taken him the distance in twenty-two title fights. He started 1998 with a perfect 46–0 record, and thirty-six of his victories have been by knockout or stoppage. That's why he is known as 'Finito', and the nickname could not be more apt. But his dream of emulating Rocky Marciano's 49–0 record was ruined in March, when he was held to a 'technical draw' when cuts forced a premature end to his unification match with WBA champion Rosendo Alvarez of Nicaragua.

He has never been beaten, having won all thirty-seven of his amateur fights. He had been a hyperactive child, who nagged his father Magdelano into taking him to a boxing gym. He was a natural, and won ten national titles before turning pro at seventeen in 1985 as the Mexican Golden Gloves champion.

Straw-weight is one of the sport's less glamorous divisions, but in Latin America and the Orient it is fiercely competitive. Lopez beat off top quality rivals to win the title, and as champion he has taken on challengers from around the world, despatching them all with the same cool precision. He is a superb combination puncher, whose balance and skill is breathtaking, but he suffers from the puncher's eternal problem of brittle hands.

In an era when too many champions insist on home advantage, Lopez has such confidence in himself that he will happily defend in the opponent's home town, including three trips to Japan and two to Korea. In a career-best showing, he stopped Thailand's Saman Sorjaturong in two rounds in 1993, yet the Thai went on to beat Humberto Gonzalez for the light-flyweight title.

Gonzalez would have been a magnificent match for Lopez, but retired rather than face his compatriot. In recent years Lopez has, belatedly, become a favourite in America where seven of his last eight title fights have been staged. Unusually for Mexican fighters, who tend to live like 1960s rock stars, Lopez is a quiet and unobtrusive man away from the ring, who would rather spend time with his fiancee Enriquta, or read a good book, than smash up the nearest bar. But no one is likely to call him a sissy ...

KENNEDY McKINNEY

Status: *WBO and former IBF super-bantamweight champion.* **Born:** *10 January 1966, Memphis*

The casual fan who thinks thrills begin and end with the heavyweight division should take a look at Kennedy McKinney. The stylish super-bantamweight has featured in more than his share of epic championship battles, including the 1996 Fight of the Year, when Marco Antonio Barrera stopped him in the final round of a WBO title bid, and his fourth-round defeat of Junior Jones for the same title in December 1997, which was so exciting that it almost stole the Madison Square Garden show from Naseem Hamed's knockout of Kevin Kelley.

McKinney's whole career has been a wild, up-and-down rollercoaster ride. He has survived drug addiction and rehabilitation, been arrested for kidnapping, won and lost the IBF title, and captured the WBO belt against the odds at an age when most men his weight would be considering retirement.

He first attracted attention by winning the US Army championship, following that with silver medals in the US and then the World amateur championships, before crowning his career by winning the gold medal at the 1988 Olympics. He barely made the team, losing a box-off against Michael Collins before eliminating Collins on a 4–1 decision in the complicated American qualifying process. Top Rank, Bob Arum's Las Vegas promotional company, snapped him up and his pro career proceeded on predictably successful lines until he tested positive for cocaine abuse and lost his licence for six months. Arum kept faith, and persuaded him to enter a rehabilitation clinic.

His troubles continued when he was arrested and jailed for the abduction of a fifteen-year-old girl, but he was later cleared of all charges and got his life back on line.

A string of impressive wins brought him his first title shot in December 1992, but he was trailing on all cards and had almost been stopped in the tenth when he rallied to knock out IBF champion Welcome Ncita of South Africa in the eleventh. He retained it three times before losing to another South African, Vuyani Bungu, in 1994. A year later he won the fledgeling WBU's belt, but never defended it and instead pursued the brilliant and unbeaten Marco Antonio Barrera, who stopped him in a classic encounter in 1996.

He finally got a rematch with Bungu in 1997, and when he lost again on points his championship career seemed over. But the irrepressible American kept plugging away, and was rewarded with that unforgettable win over Jones for the WBO title. It was his thirty-third win in thirty-seven fights (three losses, one draw) and his twentieth inside the distance.

DARIUSZ MICHALCZEWSKI

Status: *WBO and former undefeated WBA and IBF light-heavyweight champion, former undefeated WBO cruiserweight champion.* **Born:** *5 May 1968, Danzig*

His nutty heavyweight compatriot, Andrew Golota, has the bigger international reputation, for all the wrong reasons, but there is no doubt that Dariusz Michalczewski is the best professional Poland has produced. Like Golota, who emigrated to America to launch his career, Michalczewski had to leave home in 1989 and settled in Hanover, Germany. He was an outstanding amateur, taking the gold medal – representing Germany – in the 1991 European championship and winning 133 of 150 fights, 83 inside the distance. His wife Dorata joined him later that year with their two children, and Dariusz turned professional in September 1991.

His outstanding amateur pedigree meant that he was boxing in high class almost from the start, and in only his fifth fight he stopped former world title challenger Sean Mannion in three rounds. He proved almost as difficult to beat as to pronounce, and quickly developed into a strong pressure fighter with a solid chin and a heavy punch. An unbeaten run of seventeen wins, sixteen inside schedule, brought him the IBF Intercontinental title, and in the space of three months in 1994 he won WBO titles at light-heavyweight and cruiserweight. He immediately relinquished the cruiserweight belt, but up to the beginning of 1998 he had retained the light-heavyweight title ten times, with only two opponents taking him the distance.

His career-best result came in June 1997 when he took the WBA and IBF titles from the American veteran Virgil Hill, who had generally been accepted as the world's best at the weight. With three of the four major belts in his possession, he was poised to become the division's first undisputed champion since Michael Spinks twelve years previously, but instead he relinquished the WBA and IBF titles without defending them, giving the WBO a powerful propaganda boost in the process.

Michalczewski has become a big favourite with the German crowds. Strong and rugged, he maintains a relentless attack built around solid body punches, and uses a powerful straight left to set opponents up for the big rights which have brought him twenty-seven inside-schedule victories in an unbeaten thirty-six-fight career. Ten of those have come by clean countout, including five in championship fights, a strike record which even Thomas Hearns might have envied.

ORZUBEK NAZAROV

Status: *WBA lightweight champion.* **Born:** *30 August 1966, Kant, Kyrghzstan*

When the professional barriers came down in the former Eastern bloc countries, most of the leading amateurs tried their luck in the pro game but only a few made the transition successfully. Southpaw Nazarov – nicknamed 'Gussie' – was one of that fortunate handful, but given his remarkable achievements as an amateur that was no great surprise. The son of a bus driver, he started boxing at eleven and developed a distinctive style, based on body-punching, which was out of line with the traditional orthodoxy of East European amateur boxing at the time. It worked, though: he won the gold medal in the European junior championships in 1984 and the senior championships three years later, and was national champion in 1985, 1987 and 1988.

Unusually, Nazarov opted to turn professional in Japan, and won the Japanese title in his sixth fight. He took the Orient & Pacific championship in his twelfth contest and retained it five times before winning the world title, which means that sixteen of his twenty-four fights (eighteen won inside schedule) have involved championships of one sort or another. As with so many heavy hitters, his career has been severely hampered by recurring injuries, which restricted him to one fight in 1997, one in 1996, and two each in 1995 and 1994.

Nazarov has proved a good traveller. He won and retained the WBA title in South Africa, defended it three times in Japan, and stopped two fancied American challengers on their home ground. One of those was Joey Gamache, a former WBA champion at super-featherweight and lightweight who later won the WBU light-welterweight crown. Nazarov destroyed him inside two rounds, and showed just how well he has learned the professional game by insisting on a $250,000 guarantee. The show flopped, and Gamache fought for nothing. It's a cruel game, sometimes.

IKE QUARTEY

Status: *WBA welterweight champion.* **Born:** *27 November 1969, Accra*

American boxing fans are notoriously insular, which is why they have yet to warm to Ike 'Bazooka' Quartey. They took time to appreciate Quartey's compatriot Azumah Nelson, too, but Nelson won them over in the end and Quartey – real name Issifu – is likely to do the same. Now that Felix Trinidad (see below) is poised to move up to light-middleweight, the Ghanaian can claim to be the hardest hitter in the welterweight division. Unlike Trinidad, though, whose power punches come with dramatic suddenness, Quartey is more methodical in his approach, gradually breaking up opponents with steady, controlled pressure before clubbing the resistance from them.

He has knocked out or stopped twenty-nine of his thirty-five opponents, and only a disputed and controversial draw with former WBO champ Jose Luis Lopez mars his perfect record.

One of his elder brothers, confusingly also known as Ike, won the gold medal in the 1962 Empire Games, but young Ike had less luck when he competed in the world junior championships and the Seoul Olympic Games, where he boxed at light-welterweight. He turned pro on his return from Korea, and won the Ghanaian title in his sixth fight and the All-African championship in his ninth.

Opportunities are rare in Ghana, though, so he had to follow Nelson's example and go to America. A win over former American amateur star Kelcie Banks got him noticed, and the French promotional team of the Acaries brothers, Louis and Michel, took him under their wing.

He became the WBC International light-welterweight champion, but seemed to lose punching power when he moved up to welterweight and, going into his WBA title challenge to the unbeaten Venezuelan Crisanto Espana, he had been taken the distance in his last three fights. Yet he handled Espana with surprising ease, stopping him in eleven rounds, and had done the same to five of his seven subsequent championship opponents up to the end of 1997.

SAMAN SORJATURONG

Status: *WBC light-flyweight champion and former undefeated IBF champion.* **Born:** *2 August 1969, Kampangsaen, Thailand*

Oriental fighters are totally neglected by British TV companies, so the chances of seeing Saman Sorjaturong in action are slim. Yet the aggressive, hard-hitting Thai is one of the best action men in the business, offering that irresistible combination of heavy punching and vulnerability. He can take opponents out with one left hook, as has happened to twenty-eight of his thirty-six victims in thirty-nine fights (one draw) up to the end of 1997, or he can be hurt and floored himself, as when the great Ricardo Lopez blitzed him in two rounds when Sorjaturong travelled to Mexico in 1993 for his first world title chance, at straw-weight.

Sorjaturong – real name Saman Sriprateat – did nothing much as an amateur (Thais rarely do), but won fourteen in a row after turning pro on Christmas Eve, 1989. He was held to a draw in his fifteenth fight and beaten on points in a six-rounder in his sixteenth, yet after just one more win he was thrown in with Lopez. It was much too early, especially for his first trip outside Thailand, and the result was entirely predictable. Yet he hasn't lost since, in twenty-one fights, and has only been taken the distance once in nine successful world title fights.

He won the WBC and IBF light-flyweight titles the hard way, going to California to stop the respected Mexican veteran Humberto Gonzalez in seven rounds in July 1995, but relinquished the IBF belt after only one defence, a fourth-round stoppage of Japan's Yuichi Hosono, to concentrate on defending the WBC version. He has proved himself a truly international champion, repelling challengers from Mexico, Japan, Chile, South Africa, the Dominican Republic and the Philippines, although he has yet to risk defending the championship outside his home country.

JOHNNY TAPIA

Status: *WBO and IBF super-flyweight champion.*
Born: *13 February 1967, Albuquerque, New Mexico*

The adjective 'colourful' is hardly adequate to describe the extraordinary life and career of the much-tattooed Tapia. His father was murdered a few months before he was born, and when he was eight years old his mother was kidnapped, raped, hanged and stabbed twenty-two times with an ice pick.

From such a harrowing background, it is unsurprising that Tapia developed addictions to alcohol and cocaine which almost cost him his life.

He took up boxing in his hometown and won the national Golden Gloves twice, in 1983 and 1985, but then went missing for three years before resurfacing in 1988 and turning pro in March that year. One of his early trainers was Danny Romero Sr, whose son, Danny Jr, would grow up to be Tapia's great rival.

Johnny Tapia (right) on top against hometown rival Danny Romero Jr in their 1997 unification match

He settled quickly into the pro game and won his first twenty-two fights, collecting the United States super-flyweight title along the way, but then cocaine took hold and he lost three and a half years of his boxing career. He became a notorious figure in Albuquerque, and there were frequent spells in jail. But then his life turned around dramatically when, in 1993, he met and married Teresa, who now doubles as his manager. He returned to Catholicism around the same time, and eventually found the strength to kick the habit.

His boxing licence was restored in 1994, and by the end of the year he had won the WBO title, which he has held ever since. His inspiring story has made him something of a folk hero, and his showdown with IBF champion Romero in 1997 attracted interest far beyond their hometown. In fact, local police refused permission for the fight to be staged there, fearing the consequences of the rivalry between two sets of passionate supporters, and the fight was switched to Las Vegas. It passed off without incident, probably because Tapia, giving the best display of his forty-three-fight career, won beyond argument to stretch his record to 41–0–2, with twenty-five inside-schedule wins.

In all, he has won twelve title fights, and plans an assault on the bantamweight championship in 1998. His story is summed up by the Spanish words emblazoned on his ring shorts: *Mi Vida Loco* (My Crazy Life).

FELIX TRINIDAD

Status: *IBF welterweight champion.* **Born:** *Cupoy Alto, Puerto Rico, 10 January 1973*

The lanky, 5ft 11ins Trinidad is compelling viewing: take your eyes off him for a second, and you might miss a knockdown, either for or against. He is arguably the most vulnerable of the current top-grade fighters, but then he is also the best finisher of them all. His suspect defence has seen him floored frequently, notably by Yori Campas in a four-round epic in 1994 and by British champion Kevin Lueshing, but the Puerto Rican has always got up to win.

By April 1998 he had a perfect score of 33–0, twenty-nine inside the distance and boasting twelve quick wins in thirteen title fights. He didn't compile that record against soft touches, either: his beaten challengers included respected names like Oba Carr, Larry Barnes, Roger Turner, Yori Campas and the former lightweight champion Freddie Pendleton, and only the veteran Hector Camacho took him the distance.

At twenty-five, he is starting to fill out into a light-middleweight and is already installed as a contender in that division after blasting out the normally durable Australian Troy Waters in a title eliminator.

Trinidad, known as Tito, was born into the business. His father, Felix Sr, was Puerto Rican featherweight champion twenty years ago and went in the fifth round with Salvador Sanchez in 1979, a few months before the late, great Mexican won the world title. Felix Sr has trained his son since the boy was nine, and they have avoided the conflicts which so often happen in father–son boxing partnerships.

Trinidad turned pro at seventeen, and stopped eleven of his first fourteen opponents to earn a world ranking. The IBF champion at the time was Maurice Blocker, a fine craftsman from Washington, and there were fears that the title shot had come too soon for the twenty-year-old. Instead, he destroyed Blocker in two rounds, with the kind of chilling left hooks which have become his trademark.

He studied public accountancy at the University of San Juan, but dropped out when the demands of his boxing career became too much. But he has continued to study by correspondence course, and plans a career in that field when he retires from the ring.

MIKE TYSON

Status: *former undisputed world heavyweight champion.* **Born:** *Brownsville, New York City, 30 June 1966*

The raging intensity with which the young Mike Tyson demolished a whole generation of heavyweights to become the division's youngest-ever champion seemed to destine him for greatness – but then the man's own complex, tormented nature triggered the self-destruct button, and history will remember him instead for what might have been. The Tyson of the mid-1980s was like an elemental force, who somehow channelled all the violence and deprivation of his wretched ghetto upbringing into the cold, controlled fury he brought to the ring. The ghetto made him, and then it brought him down because he was unable to outgrow the twisted standards and values he had acquired as a teenage mugger on the streets of Brownsville.

Veteran trainer Cus D'Amato and his backers, Jim Jacobs and Bill Cayton, saw the fighting potential of the thirteen-year-old Tyson after Bobby Stewart, a trainer at the Tryon Schools for Boys (a last-resort establishment in which Tyson was then detained until he was sixteen) had recommended the youngster to them. Tyson was released into D'Amato's care on his fourteenth birthday, and the team set about moulding him into the perfect fighting machine. They succeeded in that, but at the cost of his social development.

They turned him professional in May 1985, and deliberately kept him off national TV until public curiosity about him reached the right level. Instead, selected influential journalists were sent videotapes of his rapidly-growing list of knockouts – eleven first-round finishes in fifteen fights in 1985 – and the publicity thus generated enabled him to take the fast track to the title. Thirteen straight wins in 1986 culminated in a second-round defeat of Trevor Berbick for the WBC title, and within ten months he had unified the various strands of the championship.

Mike Tyson was never better than in this chilling first-round annihilation of Michael Spinks

He hit his peak with an electrifying first-round knockout of Mike Spinks in 1988, but then it all started to go wrong. D'Amato and Jacobs had died, and he went through a disastrous and expensive marriage to the actress Robin Givens. Don King moved in and Bill Cayton and trainer Kevin Rooney were elbowed aside in favour of inexperienced individuals whose qualifications were as questionable as their motivation. His life was in tatters by the time Buster Douglas climbed off the floor to knock him out in February 1990, and he finally paid the price for his wildly undisciplined life-style when he was jailed for six years for raping a beauty pageant contestant.

Released in 1995, he found that his $100m fortune had somehow dwindled to $15m, but he restored it with a string of easy wins which brought him the WBC and WBA titles. But the wrong people were still around him, and there was no one with the professional expertise needed to guide him to victory over Evander Holyfield. It was even worse in the rematch with Holyfield, when he bit off a lump of the champion's ear and was disqualified, fined and banned from the sport for a year.

Early in 1998 he announced that he was leaving King and his managers, alleging financial impropriety which had, once again, wiped out the fortune he had earned on his ill-fated comeback. No doubt he will be licensed again when his suspension is completed in July 1998, and he will probably still be good enough to win a version of the title – but the chance of greatness, which once seemed assured, has gone for ever.

RECORD BREAKER

Wilfredo Gomez, the brilliant Puerto Rican, was unbeatable as WBC super-bantamweight champion between 1977 and 1982. He made a record seventeen defences, and won them all inside the distance. After relinquishing the title, he went on to win championships at featherweight and super-feather.

NAP HAND

Thomas Hearns claimed the honour of being the first to win world titles at five different weights when he outscored James Kinchen in Las Vegas on 4 November 1988 to add the WBO super-middleweight title to those he had already won at welter, light-middle, middle and light-heavy. He beat his arch-rival Ray Leonard to the record by just three days. Hearns later won the WBU version of the cruiserweight title as well.

KING DUKE

Croydon's Duke McKenzie is the only British boxer to claim world titles in three divisions: flyweight (1988–9), bantam (1991–2) and super-bantam (1992–3). He also challenged unsuccessfully for the WBO featherweight title in 1994.

CHAVEZ CASHES IN

Mexican idol Julio Cesar Chavez drew the largest paid attendance, 132,247, when he retained the WBC light-welterweight title against Greg Haugen at the Estadio Azteca, Mexico City on 20 February 1993. The record attendance with free admission was 135,132 for Tony Zale's non-title knockout of Billy Pryor at Milwaukee on 18 August 1941.

Curiously, the smallest paid attendance at a heavyweight title fight involved one of the most popular champions of all time, Muhammad Ali. Only 2,434 paid to watch him knock out Sonny Liston with the notorious 'phantom punch' in the first round of their rematch, which was staged in a high school gym in Lewiston, Maine on 25 May 1965.

CHAMPION LOSERS

Only three world champions have suffered more than fifty defeats: welterweight Fritzie Zivic (65 in 232 fights between 1931–49), lightweight Lauro Salas (52 traceable losses in 151 fights between 1946–61, although his career began in Mexico two years earlier) and light-welter Johnny Jadick (51 in 151 fights between 1924–37).

RADIO TIMES

The first live radio fight commentary featured Frankie Burns and Packy O'Gatty, who met in a preliminary bout on the Dempsey v Carpentier million-dollar show at Boyle's Thirty Acres, Jersey City on 2 July 1921. This was also the first show at which the MC used a microphone.

Britain's first broadcast was of Johnny Curley's British featherweight title defence against Harry Corbett at the National Sporting Club, London on 29 March 1926. The commentator earned his fee – the fight lasted the full twenty rounds.

It's fair to say most fans now watch most of their boxing from the comfort of their armchair.

Before the advent of television, people had to travel to watch their sport. Stadiums could accommodate more people than they can today because they were more basic, and people were in the habit of travelling to see sport as it happened. Apart from a few flickering images on cinema newsreel, the only way to see a Stanley Matthews, Dennis Compton, Jack Dempsey or Babe Ruth was to pay at the gate. Today, the brilliance of television technology makes experts of us all in our own homes.

But like everything else, boxing has become a more complex sport than it was in those pioneer years. Its rules have become more elaborate, even though its basic attraction remains that it is superficially easy to understand and appreciate: i.e. that one person finds a way of hitting the other as hard and often as possible.

However, boxing is a beautiful and often misunderstood art, which requires a great amount of technical skill for its participants to come anywhere close to perfection. Timing punches alone is difficult to master. The secrets of good footwork and perfect balance are not easily unlocked. Boxers must learn to take punches, or if possible to avoid them as economically as possible, to throw a variety of effective punches, to pace themselves over long fights, to sprint over short ones.

Above all, perhaps, boxers have to learn to think. One current champion was disqualified early in his amateur career for kneeing his opponent. It was a reaction, a response that at the time he had not yet learned to control. Yet for a boxer to make progress, he must curtail all those impulses that will take him outside the boundaries of the rules. This is not easy to master.

In a tennis match, or even when you play football or cricket, the rules are fairly easy to work within. Tempers are lost occasionally, but mostly the nature of the play means that rules are comfortably kept.

But in boxing there is an entirely different psychological playing field. Under normal circumstances, a person who is attacked will react in all manner of ways. And usually, that reaction is instinctive. He may instinctively run, or he may fight back. But beyond that, if he chooses to fight, he may use his head, his fists, his feet, his teeth, anything that occurs to him at the time.

Boxing dismantles that instinct and teaches a disciplined response. A boxer is taught to punch back correctly, with the knuckle part of the glove, on the target area. He does not kick, nor should he butt or bite. A boxer is taught, from his earliest days in the sport, that to do so is a violation of the code, of a tradition that goes back generations, and will lead to disqualification from the contest and, in severe cases, disgrace.

Boxers learn to discipline themselves, firstly in the act of boxing, and then through that, by the way they live in order to box to the highest possible level. That is why when Mike Tyson bit Evander Holyfield in their rematch in the summer of 1997, boxers themselves reacted so angrily. The public, who may excuse their heroes almost anything, tried to find excuses for him. None of the boxers I met did so. To a man they condemned him because they knew he had broken the code, that he had shown by that one contemptible act that he no longer wanted to be disciplined by boxing, or to accept what it could give him. He destroyed himself as a fighter, and destroyed himself as a role model to all those who come after him.

Mike Tyson outraged his fellow pros when he bit a lump off Evander Holyfield's ear

Above all, perhaps, fighters must learn how to lie, how to deceive opponents into believing something is real when it is not. If a fighter is hurt, he must not show it, because if he does so his hurt will be exploited. If he has hurt a hand, he must continue to throw punches with it if at all possible. As a fighter becomes more experienced, his lies become more complex.

Often a fighter who is less experienced, or who simply does not possess the understanding or intelligence to lie well enough, will smile when he has taken a hard punch. This is supposed to say 'That didn't hurt me'. But the good fighter will neither smile nor grimace. And the good fighter will know that a fighter who smiles is lying, is actually demonstrating his hurt.

Boxing has layers, and to understand it takes time. Obviously, the best place to do that is to explore it from within, by being a good boxer oneself.

But as the vast majority of us cannot experience that privilege, we can only watch as closely as possible. A seat on the ring apron is ideal, but rarely attainable. Good seats in the house are often several rows back behind banks of pressmen, VIP guests, television commentators and producers, and photographers.

Television cannot reproduce live atmosphere. However good the equipment, however proficient the operators and however knowledgeable and sensitive the commentators and analysts, pictures cannot transmit the full impact of a blow. Television sanitises boxing, sifts out the rawness of the violence. TV images cannot identify with any consistency the lies boxers tell each other. But they do give a viewer who is prepared to put in the effort the opportunity to seek out boxing's secrets and to enjoy the sport on a comparatively advanced level.

Television close-ups and slow-motion replays used well can pick apart tell-tale reactions of fighters in particular circumstances, and can sometimes give an indication of the power on view. Many of us who have spent our lives writing about boxing are used to the reaction of a newcomer who has never seen a fight from close range, who expects it to be 'like it is on the telly'. Usually, the newcomer will be shocked at the force of the punches which are thrown.

However, this apart, there is so much for the armchair viewer to unlock. What follows is an attempt to help sort out the keys.

FIGHT DISTANCES

First, fight distances. Most professional fights are over three-minute rounds. In some small shows, for example at dinner-boxing establishments where the boxing is just a part of the entertainment, two-minute rounds are still used. Probably most of the diners have little idea of the difference, and the two-minute round distance allows novice or part-time boxers a chance to earn some money without demanding of them the same standards of fitness or stamina that the three-minute round does of those a little further up the scale.

However, although two-minute rounds were popular in the 1970s and 1980s, the leading promoters of the 1990s want their boxers to work over three minutes. This view is supported by most television companies, who consider the action is more open and exciting to watch if a boxer has to work for three minutes at a stretch.

The novice distance is four three-minute rounds. From this a boxer progresses through six, eight and ten rounds. In Britain, regional title fights are ten rounds, as are national championships in many European countries. Britain, however, retains the twelve-rounds championship distance for national titles, and that is now considered the proper distance for a championship contest of any significance.

In the early part of the century, twenty rounds was the norm. By the 1930s, the fifteen-round distance was considered a fair test. After the death of a boxer in a televised contest in the fourteenth round of a contest in 1982, medical officers pushed for a reduction in the championship distance to twelve rounds. This had little basis in logic. A fighter who is susceptible to damage will certainly be more likely to suffer it when he is tired than when he is not, but damage can occur just as easily in rounds four, six and eight, as in rounds twelve or fourteen. In shorter fights, men simply fight more quickly.

The truth behind the decision to reduce rounds is perhaps more cynical: fifteen-round fights presented problems to television companies who wanted to screen them live. They did not fit into a one-hour slot. A twelve-round fight did.

WEIGHT DIVISIONS

Boxers are, or should be, matched according to level of ability and weight.

There are, at the time of writing, seventeen weight divisions, and one of the would-be governing bodies, the WBU, recognises another, the super-cruiserweight. This is far too many for purists, who would prefer to see a return to the traditional eight weight divisions from flyweight (ll2 lbs) to heavyweight (no limit). Boxing's governing bodies have not served the sport well by creating so many categories. They know that their power lies in the amount of finance they can raise, and therefore logically the more title fights they can sanction, the more power they build. The more weight divisions they can create, the more title fights they can sanction.

Something could be said in their favour if the boxers operating in them were of similar weight. However, medical opinion has led to weigh-in ceremonies being brought forward to twenty-four or sometimes as much as thirty-three hours before a contest. This is because doctors link susceptibility to brain damage to dehydration caused by reducing weight. However, the result of bringing weigh-ins forward is that now nobody really has a clue what a boxer might weigh when he actually steps into the ring.

The fact that the master of ceremonies tells us that boxer A scaled 140 lbs at the weigh-in means nothing if that weigh-in was so long ago that he has since rehydrated and eaten four square meals.

In the early 1990s an American experiment was revealing on the issue of boxers' true weights. The boxers were weighed at the normal time of twenty-four hours before the fight, and then again in the dressing room when they arrived at the arena. The disparity in the two figures was shocking – and it was found that boxers who were virtually the same weight the day before were now almost a full weight division apart. Sadly, the experiment was dropped and its findings were set to one side.

It is a problem that needs addressing, for there are always those who would exploit a situation for their own gain, but it is also reasonable to assume that most boxers fight in a weight category that suits their body, and do not attempt to 'shrink' to an unnatural poundage.

SCORING

And so, sitting at 'ringside' in your armchair in front of the TV, how do you score a fight?

In the 'bad old days', when fights were not screened live, scoring from TV was immensely frustrating because a championship fight would be cut to fill the available 'hole'. Suddenly, with a fight beautifully poised with two or three rounds to go, it would switch to the final session. In those circumstances you had no idea who had won, and had to place undue trust in the commentary team.

Now, with TV companies mostly interested in showing live fights in full, life is far less frustrating for the armchair judge.

What do you look for to see which man is winning?

Don't be afraid of marking a round even, but usually look for something that gives you a winner. Scoring, especially when a round is close, is to some extent subjective, a matter of preference for a style or a particular point of success.

But basically the traditional rules say you should try to give credit for clean punches with the knuckle part of the glove which land on target. That is, ignore slaps with the open glove, and avoid scoring a round for someone just because he has been the more aggressive. OK, so what is a punch? Some would say a tap is a punch, some argue that it is not.

Effective punching is probably a more important issue. A man can land three light jabs that will win him the round if he takes nothing in reply. But if he lands those three light jabs with no effect whatsoever, and yet takes a single, explosive left hook that sends him reeling across the ring, his senses in orbit, then who wins the round?

A judge in amateur boxing will almost certainly pick the boxer who has landed the three jabs. A judge in professional boxing will certainly pick the boxer who has landed the explosive left hook. Professional boxing demands power as well as volume. It discriminates more subtly between punch and effect. A more striking example of the difference is that in amateur boxing a knockdown counts as one punch, and is given exactly the same importance as a left jab to the face which has no effect at all.

In professional boxing, certainly at international level, extra points are usually given for knockdowns.

This conflict of volume and power is a perpetual issue, which can never be completely resolved.

One of the most famous arguments which revolved around this was in the 1987 fight between Ray Leonard and Marvin Hagler. There was no doubt that Leonard landed more punches. And equally, there was no doubt that Hagler landed the significant, heavier punches. Leonard won, but many will always argue that Hagler was robbed.

However, it is rarely so complicated. Mostly, one man has a distinct edge, either in power, in effective aggression, or in boxing skills which enable him to land far more effective blows.

Ray Leonard's middleweight title win over Marvin Hagler remains one of the most fiercely-debated verdicts in championship history

Usually, it is possible to tell who has the edge. Then it's simply a matter of adding up your card.

Most authorities now employ what is known as the 'ten-point must' system. That is, one or both boxers must be given ten points in each round. An even round will be scored ten–ten. If one boxer wins a round, but not by an especially decisive margin, then he normally gets ten points and his opponent nine.

If one boxer scores a knockdown or has his opponent in serious difficulties, then the winner gets ten, and the loser eight. If one boxer is floored twice, and on the brink of being stopped, the round may well be scored ten–seven. Most authorities do not encourage their judges to score a round any wider than ten–seven.

But remember, the winner of a round must score ten points. Therefore, if one man is knocked down once, and his opponent twice, the round might be scored ten–eight. If both are knocked down, and you think the round is even, then you should score it ten–ten. If both are knocked down, but you still feel one man did better overall work, then it is ten–nine.

If one man is knocked down, but came back and in your opinion made up the lost ground, then again, you score ten–ten. Knockdowns, under the ten point must system at least, do not necessarily mean point deductions on every occasion.

When a round is close, you may be impressed by one particular aspect of a man's work which gives him overall control of the situation.

For example, the brilliant featherweight champion Willie Pep once set out to demonstrate that he could win a round without throwing a punch. He did so by feinting his poor opponent into knots, drawing his leads and then making him miss by ridiculous distances. He dodged his rushes and made him flounder into the ropes. And he used his footwork to come forward, feinting his way in and keeping his man guessing as to which punch was about to be thrown. In fact none were, but Pep dominated psychologically to the point where it was impossible not to give him the round.

This is perhaps where a judge must be sensitive to the little sways of fortune in a fight, to the looks of panic that might cross a man's face or the sudden hesitancy. Each is a key to what is actually going on.

There have been scoring scandals, of course, for that is the nature of humanity. Corruption can occur, although in the vast majority of cases it doesn't. But some will say it is impossible to get a decision in a certain country, or even part of a country, because the officials there are biased, or under pressure from a local promoter to give his fighters the decision or face the prospect of not getting work again.

This is a problem which is addressed as time goes on. Largely the system now is better than it was, because the governing bodies insist on bringing in judges 'from the outside'. Of course, sometimes things are difficult to understand. An organisation may have a ticket-selling favourite whom it would be loath to see beaten. In those circumstances, judges can be subtly persuaded to lean a certain way.

But if they do, all we can ask is that journalists and television analysts point out the wrong-doings and lobby for things to be put right.

Basically, the armchair viewer cannot control the politics of any sport, but by scoring the fight himself he can form an opinion on what has happened on site. Having a different scorecard to an official is not as serious as it might seem at first. If your tally is 117–113 for one boxer after twelve rounds, and a judge sees it a draw at 115–115, you and he may still have agreed on ten out of the twelve rounds. But a difference in two rounds, whereby you give them by ten points to nine to Boxer A and he gives them by the same margin to Boxer B, will produce exactly that difference.

However, if you score a fight 119–111 and the judges all go for the boxer you think has lost, then something is amiss, either with your interpretation of what has happened, or more seriously, with theirs!

So much for scoring.

PICKING OPPONENTS

But who are you watching?

Stars in boxing do not usually happen overnight. Boxers do not suddenly become masters of their craft. Both are gradual processes, and promoters will want to develop their stars in televised fights to guarantee them the biggest possible exposure, while not necessarily giving them severe tests.

This can lead to what some call mismatches, where one opponent – usually the one who leaves the corner facing the camera, for it is he on whom the promoter wants the viewer to focus attention – has superior skills, desire or power to his opponent.

Promoters like knockouts, preferably dramatic ones. Television companies are not averse to them either, but they also like to see good fights, which can lead to a conflict of interest. Some promoters want to con the audience into believing they have just seen the fighting equivalent of King Kong, while the best television companies attempt to bring some sense of perspective into the situation in order to help the viewer make up his or her mind as to the validity of what they have seen.

In this way a television company can justifiably celebrate its big occasions because its viewers know and trust its sense of perspective. Promoters do not always share this view.

Promoters want people to believe in their product, that is the fighter who is, or who is being built into, a star. They want people to believe he will knock over every man he faces. And one way of doing this is to feed him on a diet of low-quality opposition.

Most television companies understand the reasons behind this, and will allow a promoter a certain degree of leeway. After all, they too are in the business of producing stars.

Consequently, a promoter can bring in a certain number of poor-quality opponents. But getting the balance right is an art in itself, for the budding star must learn more than how to knock over a man who has as much ambition as the average trench soldier in a front-line war.

Boxing trade folk identify opponents in various ways. A 'good opponent' is a man who knows his business, who will teach a young star a trick or two and take him the distance if he can. Usually, the 'good opponent' doesn't hit too hard, or take unnecessary liberties like butting or hitting low.

A promoter will usually ask an agent to bring in a particular type of opponent, depending on the stage which he feels his man is at, or depending on what he wants. Some of the less scrupulous agents will happily provide a man whom they know will try, but will be out of his depth. This often makes for good action ... and for the promoter, and television company, a 'good' knockout. Through no fault of his own, this fighter has been exploited and abused. Hopefully, he has been properly paid for the privilege.

At the lowest level, there are fighters who cannot fight, and, at the bottom of the barrel, those who have no intention of doing so. These are collectively, and cynically, called 'tomato cans' – i.e. target practice, as in objects that are lined up and fired at – bums, stiffs and tank artists (because they take dives!).

Two notoriously splendid record books of the 1980s attempted to identify habitual losers. One carried portraits of down-and-outs sleeping on park benches, alongside the name and record of the boxer, with descriptions like 'takes dives under the following names ... '.

The second carried splendid line drawings of dogs next to certain boxers. A reference to the key at the end of the book revealed that boxers with dogs next to them were believed to be boxers fighting under aliases!

Promoters and television companies usually get along in reasonable harmony. They do fall out, but generally try to work together to produce an entertaining product. And, thankfully for boxing's future, by and large they succeed.

Without the input of television exposure and financial support, a promoter cannot hope to succeed at any kind of level that will produce a workable profit. In Britain, small-hall boxing struggles along, but makes little money. In the USA, it has virtually died out. Television support has helped boxing succeed and survive, because boxing has adapted itself to the requirements of the changing times, and because it is in essence such a fascinating subject, good or bad.

THE FIGHT

And so to the night itself. What might an armchair fan miss?

Before the boxers arrive in the arena, the 'whip', employed by the promoter, allots each boxer a dressing room space. The main event boxers would normally have one to themselves, or perhaps share with a gym-mate who has an undercard slot. Undercard boxers may be separated into two rooms and divided to prevent those who are to fight each other having to prepare in the same area.

When the time comes for a fight, it is the whip who gives them the signal, or leads them into the hall. 'Whip' is a term which originated in the bare-knuckle days to describe the men who were paid to patrol the edge of the outer ring and prevent the unrulier fans from encroaching on the fighting ring itself. These officials would usually be armed with a whip or crop. After the fight, they would pass among the spectators, with whip ready to be brandished at the reluctant, to collect money for the boxers. It was known as the 'whip round', a term which has blended into the modern vernacular.

A boxer will normally need a chief second and a cut man, with the promoter providing a house second who will work a corner throughout the evening, handing up the spit bucket or water, and rinsing the gumshield. The chief second, usually the head trainer or occasionally the manager, will be responsible for motivation and tactics during the contest. The better ones say little.

A cut man is there to tend to any facial damage which might occur, and will normally leave the talking to the chief second, except for the occasional well-chosen words of encouragement. Referees tend to know good cut men and will ask their opinion of the severity of a cut. Most cut men are proud of their trade and do not take kindly to referees stopping fights when they feel they have an injury under control.

In Britain, cut men are allowed to use only still water and a coagulant solution of one part adrenalin to 1,000 water. A coagulant named Atavine is permitted in most areas of the world, but not in Britain. Over the years, cut men have used all manner of coagulants, many of which are now considered dangerous. When Matthew Saad Muhammad beat John Conteh over fifteen rounds in a light-heavyweight title fight in 1979, he had a kind of white cement jammed into a severe cut. Conteh's camp protested and the Englishman was granted a rematch.

Years ago the veteran Al Braverman famously retorted to accusations of using foreign substances on a cut. 'It's not foreign', he yelled. 'It was made right here in the US of A!'

A ring announcer can make or break a show. Selecting just the right words and delivering them in style is an art in itself which takes time to perfect. The highest-paid and best announcers of the 1990s have been Michael Buffer and Jimmy Lennon Jr, whose father was a master of the art in the

California area in the 1960s and 1970s.

Buffer's extrovert 'Let's Get Ready To Rumble' is like a statement of intent, a signal to the multitudes around the world that the big moment for which everyone has been waiting has finally arrived.

Fifty or sixty years ago, before microphones were available, or were not sufficiently powerful to make much impact on a large crowd, the ring announcer would say very little. His introductions were short and to the point, and his announcement of the decision would be along the lines of, for example: 'The winner is ... Louis. Louis.'

Modern technology allows the personality of the ring announcer to come through, and he has become an integral, and often highly paid, part of the show.

But the style of one Australian announcer, Ray Connolly, is not considered an ideal to be followed.

Introducing world champion Jeff Harding, Connolly puffed out his chest and declared that the Australian hero was 'a young man who is passionately orbiting toward catastrophic magnitude'. Harding, a wonderful Crocodile Dundee-style plain speaker, grunted later: 'Half them f...ing words I didn't even understand.' Which probably went for most of the audience as well.

Basically, however, once the bell goes, the whip, second, cut man, ring announcer, promoter and referee are, or should be, bit-part players.

The fighters are the men who matter. Enjoy the fight!

Any selection of 'the best of ...' in whatever field is necessarily personal, but few would dispute that the most consistently entertaining and stylish writer on boxing was the wonderful A.J. Liebling. The two anthologies of his work, *The Sweet Science* and *Neutral Corner*, are essential reading for devotees of American boxing in the 1950s and early 1960s. Both books, happily, are still in print.

Other worthwhile American efforts include Arlene Schulman's *The Prizefighters*, Ralph Wiley's *Serenity*, Phil Berger's *Punch Lines*, and Pete Heller's indispensable *In This Corner!* Thomas Hauser's *Black Lights* is one of the most illuminating books ever written about the business side of the sport, while his Muhammad Ali biography remains the definitive work on the man. Everett Skehan performed a similar service for Rocky Marciano, while the lives and achievements of boxing's legendary trainers are well recounted in *Corner Men* by Ronald Fried and *In The Corner* by Dave Anderson.

Harry Legge, a veteran of around 150 professional fights and countless hundreds in boxing booths, turned his experiences into two of the best British boxing books *Penny A Punch* and *For A Few Punches More*. Donald McRae's *Dark Trade* was deservedly showered with honours in 1997, and Geoffrey Beattie's *On The Ropes*, published around the same time, ran him close. The master, of course, remains Hugh McIlvanney, whose *McIlvanney On Boxing* is regularly updated and reprinted.

Many of the books listed here may be out of print, but there are excellent second-hand specialists available via the internet who also advertise in the boxing trade press.

Frank Warren's world-boxing.com
http://www.sporting-life.com/worldboxing/

Boxing.com
address: http://www.boxing.com

Naseem Hamed's site
address: http://www.princenaseem.com

Other sites:
http://www.boxing-monthly.co.uk/
http://www.squaredcircle.com/boxingtimes/98

BOXING has been ill-served by the movies, probably because the game's aura of seedy glamour and violence lends itself so easily to the grainy black-and-white (in all senses) representations offered by Hollywood in the 1940s and 1950s. The result was a string of hackneyed themes, usually involving shifty characters who can be guaranteed at some point in the story to tell the hero 'The Boss says you go in the fifth'.

But amongst the dross there have been a few worthwhile efforts, most notably *The Harder They Fall,* a bleak account of Primo Carnera's career as seen through the eyes of Humphrey Bogart as the camp's press agent, who knows what is going on but lacks the moral courage to face or expose it. The film is based on Budd Schulberg's book of the same title, and Schulberg – a lifetime fight fan whose 1995 anthology *Sparring With Hemingway* is a hugely enjoyable read – also created the unforgettable Terry Malloy character for Marlon Brando in his *On The Waterfront.* Every ex-fighter in the world can identify with Malloy in the 'coulda been a contender' scene with Rod Steiger.

In the same tradition of gritty realism, John Huston's *Fat City* captures perfectly the life of the 'opponent', the human punchbag who is always just a Greyhound Bus ride away from another hundred-dollar beating. Robert Ryan's *The Set Up* is worth a look, but too many of the rest are ludicrous tear-jerkers like *The Champ* (in its various incarnations) or Elvis Presley's *Kid Galahad* – although, curiously, Presley showed enough natural talent in the fight scenes to suggest that he could have looked after himself in the ring.

The same is true of Daniel Day-Lewis, whom former featherweight champion Barry McGuigan coached so well for his title role in *The Boxer*, but Sylvester Stallone (*Rocky*, ad infinitum) had better stick to the day job.

Paul Newman was absolutely believable as Rocky Graziano in *Somebody Up There Likes Me*, the Graziano bio-pic which launched Newman to stardom, while Robert DeNiro has never been better than as Jake LaMotta in *Raging Bull*. The fight scenes were gorily overdone, with blood dripping from the ropes, but overall it probably deserves ranking at the top of a depressingly short list of outstanding boxing movies.

ABOUT THE AUTHOR

HARRY MULLAN is acknowledged internationally as one of the world's leading authorities on boxing. He has appeared frequently on TV and radio here and in America, including stints as summariser on radio and co-commentator on television, satellite and closed-circuit broadcasts from America, Denmark, South Africa, Ireland and Britain.

His work has been featured in national papers in Britain, Ireland, Australia, America and even Hong Kong. He was boxing correspondent of the *Sunday Times* for five years, and filled the same role on the *Independent on Sunday* from 1994 until March 1998, when he left to join *Sport First*. He also contributes regularly to *Boxing Monthly*.

His books include: *The Illustrated History of Boxing* (Hamlyn, 1987), *The Book of Boxing Quotations* (Stanley Paul, 1988), *Heroes and Hard Men* (Stanley Paul, 1989), *Boxing: The Last 25 Years* (W.H. Smith, 1991), *Fighting Words* (Colebridge, 1994), *The Ultimate Encyclopaedia of Boxing* (Carlton, 1996), and *Ring Wars* (Paragon, 1997). He co-authored *Barry McGuigan: The Untold Story* (Robson, 1991) with McGuigan and Gerry Callan, and edited *A Boxing Companion* (WH Smith) with Peter Arnold in 1992. He edited *Boxing News Annual* from 1977–87, and the *News of the World Boxing Annual* from 1988–92.

He has been at ringside for many of the modern classic fights, including Hagler v Hearns, Leonard v Hearns, McGuigan v Cruz and the first two Bowe v Holyfield clashes. In all, he has covered championship boxing in eighteen countries, including over thirty major shows in Las Vegas. He is a member of the voting panel for the International Boxing Hall of Fame in New York, and is the only Honorary Life Member of the Irish Boxing Writers Club.

Married with three children and four grand-children, he lives in the village of Bridge, near Canterbury.

InsidetheGame
THE ESSENTIAL GUIDE TO SPECTATOR SPORT

This new series is designed to provide a complete overview of the major world sports for the rapidly-expanding spectator market, covering the history, the rules, the main terms, how the sport is played, the great stars and teams, the sport today and the future.

Intelligently written by leading sports journalists, the books are aimed at the passionate but discerning new sports fan. They take an alternative perspective to other sports titles, going beyond the normally bland observations and reflections of the commentator and professional sportsperson, providing readers with an informed and cliché-free framework within which to understand and appreciate the great sporting dramas.

Titles currently available:

Inside the Game: **Cricket** by Rob Steen
ISBN 1 84046 031 8

Inside the Game: **Golf** by Derek Lawrenson
ISBN 1 84046 030 X

Inside the Game: **Football** by Chris Nawrat
ISBN 1 84046 028 8

Inside the Game: **Boxing** by Harry Mullan
ISBN 1 84046 029 6

Titles for 1999:

Rugby Union, Formula 1, Horse Racing

INDEX